I WANT TO QUIT MY JOB!!

Also by Charron Monaye

BOOKS
2018 Legacy Journal & Planner: A Planning Tool for your Freedom & Future
I Matter Journal
STOP Asking for Permission & Give Notice: How To Accept & Attain Who You Are Without Validation
Love The Real You: Uncovering your "WHY" & Affirming You're Enough
UnBreak My Heart: From Scorn to Finding Love Again
My Side of the Story: From a Woman Waiting to Exhale
Bruised, Broken, and Blessed compiled by: Charron Monaye & Shontaye Hawkins

STAGE PLAYS
Get Out of Your Own Way
Why Can't We Be Friends
Living Your Life

CO-AUTHORED BOOKS
The Woodshed by: Jaguar Wright
The Shadow In My Eyes by: Deborah Rose

Books are available on Amazon, Barnes N Noble, Books A Million, Wal-Mart

I WANT TO QUIT MY JOB

8 ENTREPRENEURIAL STRATEGIES FOR MASSIVE
RESULTS WHILE EMPLOYED

CHARRON Monaye

Foreword By: Dr. Tiana Von Johnson

PenLegacy

CONTENTS

Bee Line to the Money, Head Straight to the Bank

When people think about entrepreneurship, they ultimately think you are your own boss, exclusively. But, what if I told you that employees can be entrepreneurs too! Today, technology is replacing sales representatives and budget cuts are closing businesses, sadly the "job" as we all know is slowly becoming non-existent. So, what are people replacing the average 9-to-5 with, small businesses?

Being the only African American, female, real estate broker on NYC's Wall Street, earning my first million dollars by the age of 27-years-old, I know all too well what it means to be an employee, but it was not until I became my own boss where I found my true purpose and calling. Now don't get me wrong, the job offered me job security, benefits, opportunity, and a pension, however, it took away my energy, some days my happiness and freedom of self-choice. I had to call out sick, ask permission to take a vacation, and sit at a desk for 8 hours doing what other people needed me to do. Boring, to say the least but that job prepared me for entrepreneurship. With the skills learned, talent mastered, education gained, and the networks created, I was able to quit my job well-equipped and ready for what entrepreneurship had to offer me. Yes, you read correctly, I was able to quit my job and quitting gave me the opportunity and freedom to pursue my goals and dreams, as well as make the kind of money I wanted. Not too bad for a woman from Bronx, New York.

Now I know that if you purchased this book, you are on the fence about "when to quit your job to pursue your business" or "how to work your business and gain massive results while employed." Great news, this book can offer guidance and answer both questions. I remember meeting Charron Monaye at my Master Classes "How to Build a Million Dollar Brand." She came eager and ready to learn, and at the end of the class, she took advantage and joined my coaching program. This impressed me because even though she was already a successful entrepreneur, she understood that she still needed a coach, because every successful person has one, had to invest in herself and surround herself with the right people. After our first conversation, I knew that she was serious about her brand, and the way she was managing her life as a mother, fiancé, and employee, I was amazed, but not surprised. Not surprised because she knew that her time as an employee was coming to an end and was willing to do whatever it took to plan and prepare. Planning and preparing are two of the most important steps you can take when embarking on full-time entrepreneurship. In this book, Charron gives you 8 principles on being a successful entrepreneur while being employed, so that when you quit, you can maintain and build upon that success. She also offers business and branding tips that will help you take your business and clients over the top!

Now that you are closer to your entrepreneurship journey, I want you to breathe and know that your job is your stepping stone for what you envision for yourself, and quitting is around the corner. This book is filled with truth, transparency, and techniques used by many employees turned entrepreneurs. We all were given the blueprint to transition, and now Charron Monaye is passing that blueprint on to you. But, please know, you only get what you put into this journey. Now get to work and start drafting your resignation letter.

Dr. Tiana Von Johnson

Visit Tiana online TianaVonJohnson.com and follow her on Social Media @TianaVonJohnson

ABOUT TIANA VON JOHNSON

Million-dollar branding expert Dr. Tiana Von Johnson is living the life that she loves. Using her extraordinary gifts and skills, Tiana developed a significant following among aspiring entrepreneurs and celebrities who seek her wisdom on building million-dollar empires. After walking away from her 9-to-5 job at 27-years-old, she started her own business and generated over $1 million dollars in her first year. Today she coaches entrepreneurs and celebrities, speaks around the country and gives back through her nationally distributed magazine and organization, Women Doing It Big.

2009

✓ December 5, 2009 - Started writing journey at Kandi Burrus's event in Atlanta, GA.

2011

✓ Wrote lyrics for ML The Truth's song "Commitment", which was later considered for a Grammy Award in the category Best R&B Song.
✓ Became a published author; *My Side of the Story* released under Purposeful Publishing.

2012

- ✓ Recognized as Outstanding Contribution to Poetry by Great Poets Across America.
- ✓ Wrote and co-produced first theatrical production, *Living Your Life*.
- ✓ Released second book, *Living, Loving, &Laughing My Way Through*.

2013

- ✓ Honored in Cleveland, OH by the organization Girls on Fire; received the Presidential Award and Best Independent Author Award.
- ✓ Wrote and produced theatrical production, *Why Can't We Be Friends*.

2014

- ✓ *Why Can't We Be Friends*, an anti-bullying play, won Best Real-Life Drama Stage Play at the Playwright Awards in Queens, NY.

2015

- ✓ Became an Amazon Best-Selling Author with third release, *Love the Real You,* published under Pen Legacy Publishing.
- ✓ Pen Legacy Publishing officially opened for business, signingthree new authors: Summer Willow Fitch, Vaughn McNeill, and La'Mena Marie

2016

- ✓ Released fourth book, *STOP Asking for Permission & Give Notice.*
- ✓ Published new author AJ Harrison.
- ✓ Hired to write two theatrical productions, *Oliva Lost & Turned Out* and *Til Death Do U Part.*
- ✓ Completed formal training through Dimensioned Wellness, LLC; became a Life Coach.

2017

- ✓ Named "Woman Who Is Doing It Big" at Millionaire Mogul, Tiana Von Johnson's Women Doing It Big Conference in New York City.
- ✓ Co-wrote memoirs with Neo-Soul Singer/Songwriter Jaguar Wright and Philadelphia Police Officer Deborah Rose.
- ✓ Published four new authors: Deborah Rose, Jaguar Wright, Briana McKnight, and Khristina Barnes.
- ✓ Hired to write two theatrical productions, *Testify* and *Cheatin' In the Next Room.*
- ✓ Pen Legacy officially registered as a Limited Liability Corporation and trademarked.
- ✓ Participated in the Literary Takeover Book Signing in New Orleans, LA, during Essence Festival.
- ✓ Studied "Writing for Television" under television producer, screenwriter, and author Shonda Rhimes.
- ✓ Received professional recognition and endorsement from Word of Life Christian Fellowship; appointed as "Fellow

of the Most Excellent Order of International Experts (FOIE)" in the field of Entrepreneurship.
- ✓ Received Honorary Doctorate Degree in Philosophy from CICA International University & Seminary.
- ✓ Became an Amazon Best-Selling Author with fourth book, *STOP Asking for Permission & Give Notice.*
- ✓ Brand advertised in a digital marketing billboard campaign in Times Square– Manhattan, NY.
- ✓ Rise and Grind Ambassador for Shark Tank's Daymond John's newest book, *Rise and Grind.*

2018:

- ✓ Theatrical production *Get Out of Your Own Way* premieres in Hollywood, CA.
- ✓ Released co-authored book, *Bruised, Broken & Blessed,* introducing thirteen new authors.
- ✓ Studied writing and editing techniques under NAACP Image Award-winning author Victoria Christopher Murray.

Remember, it's not about quitting your job, but using your job for leverage until your…

"Side job becomes your day job!"

Introduction

Steve Harvey said, *"You gotta jump to be successful."*

Lisa Nichols will inspire you to *"embrace your imperfections, beat procrastination, and 'leap afraid' – So you can take action in spite of your fears."*

Danielle Steel said, *"Sometimes, if you aren't sure about something, you just have to jump off the bridge and grow your wings on the way down."*

Les Brown says, *"Shoot for the moon. Even if you miss, you'll land among stars!"*

You may be asking yourself, "What is this 'jump' everyone is referring to? What exactly am I soaring towards?"

When starting out on my entrepreneurial journey, I can remember listening to Oprah Winfrey say, *"Everybody has a calling. And your real job in life is to figure out as soon as possible what that is, who you were meant to be, and to begin to honor that in the best way possible for yourself."* Those words played over and over in my head. I realized in order for me to figure out my calling, I had to "jump". Or in other words; I had to step outside my comfort zone. I had to stop depending on others to validate my vision and start believing I could be the success story I saw for my life.

My Personal Jump

In 2009, I was a mother of two boys, recently divorced, temporarily employed, and had no savings account. Desperate for a miracle, those words spoken by Oprah replayed in my mind, causing me to consider utilizing my gift of being a writer. I didn't know how I would fund the books I wanted to publish, but remaining silent and unfulfilled was taking me nowhere fast. Better yet, my closets were becoming cluttered with all of my composition books and journals full of stories and poems that were collecting dust. Like many people, I sat on my talents because I didn't think people would be able to relate. In my mind, I was the only single mother in existence struggling to make ends meet. Plus, I could not see myself sacrificing the little money I had on a dream that may never come true.

However, in that moment, I was on the living room floor crying, trying to convince myself, "You can only go up from here."

Eventually, I stood up…

Declared it was time to be great! It was time to share my story and see if I was the only woman in the world with problems. I started posting on social media about songwriting opportunities because I knew poems were actually song lyrics. One day, Cymande Coburn of 912 James Street Productions from Douglasville, Georgia, replied to one of my posts and asked me about writing songs for his artist. He sent three instrumental tracks and said, "Can you get reference tracks done with your lyrics and send them back to me?"

I jumped up and down with joy, but then I realized I couldn't sing and didn't have access to a studio. What to do? So, thinking quick, I called my college friend and sorority sister, Summer Willow Fitch. After telling her about the opportunity and my dilemma, she said without hesitation, "Latrese and I will reference them, and I have a studio we can use." I immediately grabbed my laptop and sent her the poems/lyrics along with Cymande's three tracks. "You will have the reference tracks back in about two weeks," she told me.

O.M.G! Is this opportunity really happening? I thought to myself. I cried like a baby when I got off the phone with her, because I knew between my lyrics and their voices, Cymande would hire me as an in-house lyricist.

Two weeks later, I was listening to my newly created songs, "Just Friends", "Better with Me", and "Lonely Days". After listening to them about six times, I emailed him the songs. About thirty minutes later, he called me yelling, "Yo, Charron! I love these! Welcome to 912 James Street Productions."

Is this really happening?
Yes!
But I don't know anything about the business.
Uh-oh.

It isn't a secret that the music industry is a cut-throat and vicious business. I called my homie Hassan, who had previous management experience in the industry, and he decided to represent me. Together, we got to work. He got tracks. I got to writing. Summer and Latrese got to referencing. Our hustle was on point, and my promotion skills landed me an opportunity to attend Xscape member Kandi Burruss's Meet and Greet in Atlanta, Georgia. December 3, 2009, we drove…well; he drove from Philadelphia to Atlanta to attend her event. This opportunity gave me the platform to get in front of the who's who in the industry.

Just think, I went from crying on my floor while trying to figure out life as a single mother with no money, to traveling to attend Kandi's event in Atlanta. WOW! Still broke, but now broke with opportunities.

When we arrived in Atlanta, we met up with Cymande to discuss business and the future of Charron Michelle and 912. It was a very productive meeting and the beginning of my jump. December 5th, it was showtime! This day not only put me in a room with ATL's finest, it's also the day when I said *"I DO"* to my writing career. My days of dreaming were over. It was time to bring it.

As we stepped in the building, it was crowded. Cameras, drinks, music, fans, and security guards filled the space. "You got this, "Cymande told me. Hassan and I had our prep talk, as we always did before important meetings, and I replaced my groupie mindset, becoming the aspiring writer who wanted to work with Kandi. I had my business card *and* demo CD with me.

As we moved further into the building, I realized there was another room. As I peeked in, I noticed there were more

people, cameras, drinks, music, and security guards. This time, while scanning the room, I spotted Kandi Burrus, Rasheeda Buckner-Frost, Toya Wright, and Diamond.

I told Cymande and Hassan that was the room I was supposed to be in, to which Hassan replied, "Remember what I told you and get it."

I nodded in agreement, showed the security guard my pass, and went in the room to mingle with Kandi and the ladies.

Mission Accomplished!

I got the opportunity to meet and chat with Kandi, take pictures, and drop off my demo.

After leaving the room, I became super nervous. That's when the doubt set in, and I started worrying if she would like it or even listen to it. But then, my oldest son Chris called to tell me that he broke the board and got promoted to yellow belt. He was so excited and expressed to me that we were both winners. I cried from excitement and guilt. I was excited that my son accomplished his goal, but I was upset and felt guilty for not being there to witness it and show support. When I told Chris about my conversation with Kandi and passing my demo to her people, he became even more excited. "Mommy, she will love it, and if she doesn't, you will make it without her," he said.

How does my son have more faith than me?

After I hung up with him, I walked back to Hassan and Cymande to share the great news with them, and we continued to enjoy the festivities.

By the end of the visit, I had secured the opportunity to write for R&B artist ML the Truth from Jackson, Mississippi. He had the perfect voice for a song I was working on called "I Apologize". So, that deal was sealed. Once I returned to Philadelphia, ML and I got to work. I sent him the lyrics to "I Apologize", and what he returned to me was the most amazing song ever! His voice. My lyrics. We were the new Ashford and Simpson, just not in a relationship or married. He knew how to convey the message in my words. I felt like he got me, like he could totally relate to my words. Then, to my surprise, he invited me to come to Jackson to work on more songs for the release of his upcoming commercial album, *The Truth.*

I flew to Jackson to meet him and get to know the person who I was working with. We went to the studio to meet another one of his producer friends, Howard, and see what music he had. Howard was playing a track that I fell in love with. It was a ballad, and it spoke to me. The words were writing itself in my head as the music played. I asked Howard if I could write the lyrics for it, and he responded, "Absolutely." He emailed the track to ML, and I promised to make him happy with the creation.

After my tour of Jackson and eating some of the best soul food I've ever had, we returned to ML's house and went to work on the track. ML had a studio in his home, so I was able to get cozy on the couch with the most comfortable blanket and started writing. He let the track play over and over again until I handed him the lyrics. He read them, then went into the booth and started singing. Two and a half hours later, the song "Commitment" was fully recorded! This song changed my life and landed us consideration for a Grammy Award. Plus, both of my songs I wrote, "I Apologize" and "Commitment", were included on his album.

Just when I thought it couldn't get any better, I landed a book publishing opportunity with Purposeful Publishing in St. Louis, Missouri. The remaining poems I did not adapt into songs were placed in a manuscript. Everything was moving really fast, but I was enjoying it because a writer is who and what I am.

While my dreams were coming to fruition, I knew it was time to get my professional and personal life in order. My fraternity brother told me that his job was hiring and offered to give my résumé to his friend in human resources. I handed over my professional portfolio to him and prayed for whatever opportunity his connection could extend. At the time, I was working part-time as a paralegal at Bell & Bell LLP. Even though I loved my job, I had new dreams and expenses that needed full-time money. One day while at work, the HR rep from the Department of Veterans Affairs called to schedule me for an interview. A week later, I went to the interview. Two days after the interview, they called and offered me a full-time position as a Veterans Service Representative.

I accepted.

Now being a federal employee, I needed to change my name in order to keep my personal life separate from my entrepreneurial life. As a public servant, I did not want my writing or work to be viewed as politically incorrect and risk running into ethical issues. So, Yolanda, who was my book publisher, and I decided it would be a good idea to create a pseudonym to use as my author name. Before this, I went by my real name, Charron Michelle. Dropping my first name was out of the question, so I focused on coming up with another middle name. I wanted something that linked me to money and France because my dream is to go to Paris. I walked around my room saying money in different variations. I pronounced it with different accents and flares. Then I said, *Monaye*. I looked up its meaning, and to my surprise, I learned that Monaye is French. When I googled it, links about money came up. From that point, the pseudonym Charron Monaye was born and my life as an author began.

I took all my poems that I had not turned into lyrics and created a book of every emotion, situation, and dream of a little girl, woman, and mother. Even though I still thought I was the only one trying not to struggle, I wanted to believe I was wrong, especially since my lyrics were winning in the music industry.

When my first book of poetry titled *My Side of the Story* was released on February 1, 2011, the responses and amount of support that I received surprised me. I could not keep a book on hand at the house, in the car, or on my bookshelf. The success of this book gave me the fuel to jump more often and further than ever before. Since then, I've jumped to become a playwright and producer in 2012, the founder and book publisher of Pen Legacy in 2015, an entrepreneurial coach in 2016, and have received an Honorary Doctorate's Degree in 2017 from CICA International University & Seminary, all while employed and writing books.

Impressive, right? I am still amazed at how much I've accomplished in my writing career. Many people ask, "How do you do it all, especially with a full-time job and children?" It's not easy, but within this book, I will share the eight strategies I used to transition from working the business to being the business, all while clocking in at a job outside of my home. In addition, I will offer ways to prepare for your resignation if quitting your job to seek entrepreneurship full-time is your desire. Quitting your job unprepared is a disaster, and as your coach, I will help prevent that from happening.

Do Not Quit Your Job Tomorrow

Let's make one thing clear; this book is about being comfortable with pursuing your entrepreneurial journey while still employed. I am *not* encouraging you to quit. This book is geared toward dismantling the myths that say you can't pursue your dreams while employed. It will give you the tools and resources needed to successfully build your business while working your nine-to-five. Some people will tell you quitting is the only option to building and planting the seeds to success.

False!

I know a lot of successful entrepreneurs and celebrities who are both employees and business owners. Entrepreneurship is hard and nothing within it is guaranteed, not even clients and on-time payments. So, in today's society, you need a plan B, C, D, E, F, all the way to Z. As you read above, I acquired opportunity after opportunity, but I never mentioned cashing million-dollar checks or anything remotely close to it. My job provided me, and still gives me, the capital necessary to keep traveling and pursuing my dreams. So, before youmove forward and make a drastic decision, know this; you can be an employee and entrepreneur. Entrepreneurship is challenging, and what you think will happen probably won't come about right away. So, give it time. In due time, though, everything you desire *will* evolve.

What to Expect from this Book

Quitting your job is the ultimate goal, but it takes consistent work and the implementation of strategic moves before you can draft that resignation letter. *I Want to Quit My Job* is the entrepreneurial manual to achieving what may seem impossible and attaining success based on the most important lessons I've learned along my journey. These lessons, or what I would like to call strategies, are the heart of this book and relevant to any person who is looking to build a business or elevate their already existing business. The first chapter will breakdown the employee vs. entrepreneur syndrome, which will provide you with the pros and cons and further explain why getting prepared for entrepreneurism while employed is essential. The remaining chapters delve into one strategy apiece. The eight strategies for massive results while employed, in order, are:

- Understanding the Purpose
- Executing The Business Set-Up 101
- Remaining Committed to the Goal
- Your Employer is your First Investor, Capitalize on it!
- How to Balance Time and Family with No Time Left in A Day
- Self-Care Leads To Great Wealth
- How to Pay For The Ultimate Sacrifice
- Zero Capital & Bad Credit…. What To Do???

In addition, I am offering "I Want to Quit My Job Entrepreneurial Conversations" with fellow entrepreneurs from all over the world who have either remained employed while being an entrepreneur or fired their boss to pursue entrepreneurship full-time. These conversations are meant to bring to life what I am sharing in this book, while giving you other lessons and experiences on how to reach your goals. At times, it is not always enough to learn from only one person, because they may not be in the same industry as you or share your same passions. However, with this diverse panel of women, I am sure you will receive the advice or guidance you are looking for. I did not provide the "I Want to Quit My Job Entrepreneurial Conversations" participants with any information regarding the book. This way, I could be ensured that they spoke from a place of transparency.

This book is not about academics; it is based on my own personal journey of achievements and failures. It is hard to inspire others to achieve what you have not already achieved yourself. So, while reading, keep in mind that I have lived, completed, and learned every story, question, and result printed in this book. This book is affectionately known as my playbook to a successful life doing what I love while doing what I have too.

Who Should Read This Book?

I Want to Quit My Job: 8 Entrepreneurial Strategies for Massive Results While Employed is for doers, influencers, and achievers who know that living in a one-dimensional world is ineffective. By one-dimensional, I mean waking up, going to work, coming home, eating dinner, and going to sleep...then repeat. Living a life without fulfilling your purpose or dream is a life unlived, and those individuals who are ready to live life will benefit the most from what I will share. If you are someone who is set in the employee ways, this book will challenge your mindset when it comes to entrepreneurship.

By no means am I discrediting employment. I am, however, encouraging the power of having something you own. Just like many financial gurus praise homeownership because the home is yours and gains equity, entrepreneurship gives the same perks. With the proper effort and investment, it gains equity and it's yours. Just like you can lose your house, you can lose your business. The goal is to be fully educated so your legacy can out live you and become a family inheritance and wealth builder for generations to come. Your place of employment can never be considered a legacy that you can leave behind, because once you die, your desk and workload are immediately reassigned to someone else. We, at Pen Legacy, LLC, are all about living and leaving legacies. As much as we promote jobs, we also encourage entrepreneurship.

What Does This Book Require from You?

This adventure will require a lot of risk-taking and courage. I am going to ask you to complete challenging questions to help provoke mind-shift thinking. There will be times where I may say something that goes against everything you believe to be true, but know that your breakthrough is on the other side of old theory. Lastly, I am going to ask for your honesty. You will never be able to write your resignation letter if you try to trick yourself into thinking you're ready when you know you're not. Your ability to live the life you envision for yourself is determined by the amount of knowledge, investing, and consistency you apply to the process while respecting the process. As long as you know that quitting your job will not be something you will do overnight or by the time you finish reading this book, you will not set yourself up to be disappointed. By accepting that failure is a part of success, you will remain committed to the journey. Knowing that you can't achieve your goals of entrepreneurship alone, you will remain mentally and emotionally sane.

So, if you are ready to build a legacy, let's get started.

"I Want to Quit My Job"
Entrepreneurial Conversation...

Vanessa Mbamarah is an entrepreneur and philanthropist with an enthusiasm for empowerment, creativity, and digital technology. She is proactive with a great sense of responsibility for self and her immediate environment. She is from Nigeria but residing in Cotonou, Republic of Benin.

Orphaned at a very delicate time of her life and being a single mother with three siblings to raise alone, Vanessa's passion of becoming a pillar of support for other children and women passing through similar experiences was kindled, leading to the creation of her foundation. She is the Founder/President of Love a Child Foundation, a non-profit humanitarian organization that is dedicated to reaching out and showing love to street and orphaned kids in Cotonou, Benin.

With LAC, she aims to give back the love she missed out on, return smiles on their faces, and show the world that every child deserves to be loved regardless of who they are and where they come from.

"I believe in empowerment and mentoring others, giving people the opportunity to be who they want to be regardless of gender or background. I also believe it is our responsibility to

encourage other people towards making something out of their lives." – Vanessa Mbamarah

Contact Info:
Website: http://ztallion.com
Email: vanessa@ztallion.com

Tell us about your business (es).

I am the Founder and Creative Lead at Ztallion, a creative digital agency specializing in branding, web design, and digital marketing - focused on delivering unique, impactful, and memorable brand experiences, alongside providing creative and strategic solutions to help businesses.

After undergoing the Digital Skills training by Google in 2016 and becoming a trainer, I pioneered the Digified Bytes Training Program in Cotonou, an initiative of Google to train onemillion Africans on digital marketing. In April 2017, I was selected as one of Google's Success Stories before officially becoming the Official Training Partner for Google's Digital Skills for Africa (DSA) Training Program in Francophone Countries, focused on providing digital skills trainings to business owners.

In September 2017, I was selected to participate at the Google Business Groups (GBG) Summit in Singapore as the Woman Lead under the Women will by GBG representing Benin Republic. With this, I aim to bridge the gap between women and the digital world, thereby allowing them to take responsibility and become better managers of their businesses or creators of new business ventures. With a passion for transfer of knowledge and empowering others, I am currently setting up the Ztallion Academy, a platform designed for young entrepreneurs and business professionals who are passionate about digital and want to leverage on it to build authority, gain more visibility, and build digital businesses.

After quitting your job, did you ever have to become an employee again to make ends meet while business was slow? Why or Why Not?

No, I did not! However, I must confess it wasn't easy. At one point, I almost turned back to the 9-to-5 world, but I had bigger dreams and knew I could only get there following the entrepreneurial path. Most importantly, I needed the freedom to explore all I was capable of doing and taking advantage of all that was available to me at that time of my life. Working a 9-to-5 sure didn't give me that space.

Do you agree or disagree with this statement? In order for me to be fully successful in my business, I must quit my job. Please explain.

Before quitting your job, it's advisable to have in place a follow-up plan and enough resources to keep you going until it starts bringing in cash. If you don't have that, don't quit just yet. But, if you got all that in place and have done all you need to do to get started, then yes! Your new business is going to be your new baby for the next couple of months, and it needs all of you to make it work.

Before you resigned from your job, what financial resources did you have in place that helped you prepare for your resignation?

For me, I quit my job at a wired time. I had saved up some cash, but it sure wasn't enough. That I found out later on. If I knew then what I know today, I'd have made better choices. First, I would have started off with a side business and grew that until it was stable enough for me to leave my 9-to-5. Secondly, I would have started building a financial portfolio and investing before resigning to start my own.

Being an entrepreneur, how do you balance life and family when there seems to never be enough time in a day?

You got that right! There is never enough time to finish all the work that needs to be done, especially when you're just starting out as a new business owner and a single parent. It can all be overwhelming, but prioritizing is key. Knowing what's relevant and what's not. For me, being available for my little one came top on my list. So, finding time to be there for her was priority.

During your journey as an entrepreneur, what have you had to sacrifice so you can remain self-employed?

Being a single mom, I had no choice but to go head on and do all I could to succeed. Apart from cutting off visits to the shopping malls (*hahaha*), I had to focus on what was most important, which at that point was building and surviving. Taking that journey for me meant sleepless nights and putting in the extra hours, which meant time away from friends and little time to do all the things I loved doing.

What advice would you give someone who is planning to quit their job to seek entrepreneurship full-time?

First of all, ask yourself, "Why? Why do I want to become an entrepreneur? "Being able to answer that question, I believe, will help you remain focused even when the journey gets rough. Apart from that, having a financial backup plan to keep you going for a few months after you leave your job is paramount and a stress reliever. If you want to win and have a successful business, start building even while still employed.

The 8 Entrepreneurial Strategies

Your day job should finance your side job, until your side job becomes your day job. But, in the meantime, you have to operate as if your side job is your day job.
~ Dr. Syleecia Thompson

Strategy #1:
Understanding the Purpose

When I started my entrepreneur journey, I did not know my destination. I just knew I had been through enough stuff that I had to release it. I literally took poems and created lyrics. I took dialogue and wrote scripts. I had no idea I was building a business or creating a platform that would be entrepreneurial in concept. I was using my passion to earn money. Period! I was a broke, single mom who needed money and fast. Instead of complaining about my situation, I used my gift and made it work for me. However, as I educated myself on the business and grew to learn my own capabilities, my quest for making money converted back to what writing started out as for me...therapy. Being someone who has always been silent about her feelings and emotions ever since I was a child, I found refuge in my pen and peace in sharing my truths on paper, which could not talk back to me. I could write without hearing the opinions, thoughts, and suggestions of anyone. The only voice I heard was my own. How cool was that?

So, I used writing as a means of release and peace, but being an author, I wanted to give the purpose more depth. How could I connect to my readers while remaining true to my voice? How was I going to handle their feedback and reviews? Then eventually, I learned my community. I read their posts, learned the common issues, and used that to leverage my writing. Doing this gave me relevancy and the ability to write about my experiences, education, success, and failures in the areas most people were struggling in, such as finances, healthy relationships, entrepreneurship, self-love, and disarming the need of validation. With each new element I mastered, I would write a book to share. The crazy thing is, my books were written to share my experiences, success, and lessons to make life easier for others, but they also served as playbooks for myself. You know how pastors say, "I am preaching to myself"? Yup! That became my books. I literally was telling myself what I needed to hear, along with teaching others everything I knew on living their best life. It was almost like God planted my own answers in me as I was writing. My writing took on a dual purpose: direct others to success while healing myself from failure.

Whether you're an employee or an entrepreneur, understanding your ultimate goal is very important. It puts the question, *"Why am I doing this?"* in perspective. You would be surprised how many people are working a job or building a business, and not clear on the purpose of it or where the opportunity will take them. I used to sit and think, "How is this possible?" Who works a job day in, day out and have no plans on what's next. Doing the same job year after year is stagnate behavior to me. How are you growing? What new skills are you obtaining?

I am a firm believer that every opportunity is a stepping stone toward something better, but you have to move to grow. This is most pertinent to my college graduates. I have two degrees (BA in Political Science & Masters in Public Administration) and two certificates (Paralegal & Life Coaching). So, why would I use only 20% of what I know when I have 9½ years of higher education and expertise to contribute to the world? In addition, I am paying 100% of my student loans and not being paid for 100% of what I know. Think about it! If you have a degree, how many of your classes or prior experiences do you contribute to your job every day? If you are like many, you are not even working in your field of expertise. You have a degree in law but working in IT. Go figure! This is why knowing your purpose in life is so necessary. It's time to grow and evolve, while utilizing every fabric of who you are.

Challenging Questions

What Are Your Short-term & Long-term Goals?

Short-term Goals

_____

_____

_____

_____

_____

_____

_____

Long-term Goals

_____

_____

_____

_____

_____

_____

_____

How old do you want to be when you retire? How are you preparing to make sure this happens?

_____

_____

_____

_____

_____

_____

_____

What is the purpose of you going to work everyday?

_____

_____

_____

_____

_____

_____

_____

What is the purpose of you being an entrepreneur? What purpose will it serve?

_____

_____

_____

_____

_____

_____

_____

What is hindering you from pursuing your dreams?

_____

_____

_____

_____

_____

_____

Knowing the answers to these questions are vital to you living the life you envision. Plus, it allows you to prepare and plan ahead. Working with no plan in place is why many people feel overworked but not accomplished. Have you ever thought to yourself, I did all of the work but really haven't accomplished anything? You are no better now than you were when you first started. In addition, knowing the "why" makes the "how-to" or "what's next" a little easier to obtain. In my experience of being an employee and/or entrepreneur, I've noticed that when people discover their "why", they are more prone to executing and achieving promotions and job changes. The same goes in life, period! For example, when people realize they need a car for accessibility and independence, they apply for loans and go to the car dealership to see what their money can buy. When they want to purchase a house, they start cleaning up their credit and saving for the downpayment. When they want to lose weight, they get on a diet, go to the gym, or both. These examples are like people who want to pursue entrepreneurship. Some pursue for profit and others for passion, but they start with an end goal in mind.

Now some "whys" or goals will not be so easy to obtain because the "how-to" is not fully understood, thus requiring further education and accountability coaching. When I first started my writing career, I did not need formal education or coaching on writing. However, I did need guidance regarding the industry. I came to the table knowing how to write, but I did not understand how to get my book published or how to get book sales. So, I had to learn publishing, both traditional and self-publishing, as well as selling and promoting books. Some people made this look extremely easy, but when you are just starting out, knowing how to identify and reach your target audience seems impossible. So, I took to Google and learned. In addition, I attended a lot of free webinars and became friends with many published writers and industry people on social media. Through their knowledge, I was able to understand the basics, which saved me some headaches. However, it wasn't until I actually started up the publishing tree that I realized it was time to invest in a coach.

In 2014, I joined Dr. Syleecia Thompson's visionary coaching group on Facebook. Syleecia is a professor at Berkeley College, business owner, serial entrepreneur, and the older sister and manager of R&B diva Syleena Johnson. Plus, she is a member of Zeta Phi Beta Sorority, Incorporated. Z-Phi! In her group, she coached and finally streamlined my writing journey to reflect who I am and what my ultimate goals are. It wasn't enough that within six years, I had authored two books, adapted two of my poems into songs that were placed on a commercial album, written and produced two stage plays, was considered for a Grammy Award, and the co-author of five book anthologies. All of that meant nothing to anyone because I had no business in place and no one really knew of my success besides friends and family. I had loyal customers who purchased my work, but for the amount of money I was spending, their money did not help me break even. Thank God for my job, because I was always two seconds away from filing bankruptcy and being evicted. My paycheck had to take care of my children and personal expenses, while also being the capital for my writing. Collectively, I was not making that much after taxes.

Syleecia gave me the right information and plan to execute my purpose, and by the end of 2014, I was blessed to watch my gift of writing transform into a full business, Pen Legacy. Through her coaching, I learned the key elements of business, how to brand and market my business, how to write a business plan, selecting a business structure, and the act of pitching. It may seem like a lot, but it's the bases to building and constructing your business.

Strategy #2:
Executing The Business Set-Up 101

According to the Small Business Association, only two-thirds of small businesses survive past two years. It's a roller coaster ride, so you must love what you're doing in order to survive the ups and downs. While creating my blueprint of Pen Legacy and Charron Monaye "The Author", I created my strategy based on my answers to these questions:

- What product or service will you offer?
- What will your budget be?
- How much will you charge?
- Who is your target audience?
- What problem are you solving?

Being clear about my business and my budget enabled me to research, register, and start operating my company properly. In the spring of 2015, I launched Pen Legacy Publishing, a small press company, and my first client was Summer Willow Fitch. I published my third book, *Love the Real You*, and her book, *Let Me Tell You Like I Told Myself:*

Love's Truth Never Changes. This business venture not only gave me the ability to publish my own books, but also the opportunity to help others fulfill their dream of becoming an author. However, before I could really roll out this new venture, I had to make sure I completed these nine things to ensure legitimate success:

- ✓ Conduct market research.
- ✓ Write a business plan.
- ✓ Fund business.
- ✓ Pick a business location.
- ✓ Choose a business structure.
- ✓ Choose a business name.
- ✓ Register business.
- ✓ Get federal and state tax IDs.
- ✓ Open a business bank account.

Launching new ventures without these things in place will make for chaos, potential tax invasion, possible lawsuits, and not being seen as trustworthy. If you are ready to pursue your business, start the process of deciding and pursuing these things during your lunch break and/or over the weekend. The great thing is you can do most of these processes using the internet, leaving no excuses as to why you can't get stuff done.

As you read this book, you will see that there is a lot of administrative work that should be completed before you launch and execute a business, regardless if it's a solo or joint venture. Now, some entrepreneurs will say you can operate a business with only accomplishing about three to five things on that list, but I advise you to do them all before you start promoting to the public. Now there are exceptions to every rule. Some small businesses don't require you to complete everything in advance, but I always try to get everything on the list done first so I can focus on what's next on my to-do list. Nothing is worse than having to go back to file paperwork or setup business strategies midway through launch or afterwards. If you need help completing any of the small business requirements, you can always contact me, a tax or business professional.

Branding

Now that you have your small business requirements in order, it's time to brand your business. This is the heartbeat of your business. If this part is not in alignment with who you are, it will be quite a challenge for you to have a successful business. Before we move forward, let's define branding according to *Entrepreneur Magazine*:

Branding is your promise to your customer. It tells them what they can expect from your products and services, and it differentiates your offering from that of your competitors. Your brand is derived from *who you are, who you want to be, and who people perceive you to be.*

Branding is ultimately an image (you) or product (business) that is contained in a bigger business or service that generates ASSETS. See why I say branding is the heartbeat of your business? It is the core that separates you from your competitors and other relatable messages within the marketplace. If you notice, there are a lot of companies that share the same purpose and items, but they differentiate themselves by their logo and business tagline (a memorable, meaningful, and concise statement that captures the essence of your brand). Your website, packaging, and promotional materials should integrate your logo and communicate your brand. Your brand strategy is how, what, where, when, and to whom you plan on communicating and delivering your brand messages. Where you advertise is part of your brand strategy. Your distribution channels are also part of your brand strategy. What you communicate visually and verbally are part of your brand strategy, too.

The 4 P's of Branding

- **Purpose** ~ What's the purpose of your company?
- **Products** ~ What can you offer people to further learn from or engage with after your services or conversation is over?
- **Packaging** ~ What makes your items or services appealing?
- **Pricing** ~ Are you pricing competitively in the marketplace? If you are pricing high, what makes it worth the value?

Defining your brand is like a journey of business self-discovery. It can be difficult, time-consuming, and uncomfortable. It requires, at the very least, that you answer the questions below:

- What is your company's mission?
- What are the benefits and features of your products or services?
- What do your customers and prospects already think of your company?
- What qualities do you want them to associate with your company?
-

This step may require you to hire a brand strategist like Dr. Tiana Von Johnson. Even though Syleecia taught me about branding, having another coach to see your business from a different eye can truly help elevate your brand. Dr. Tiana Von Johnson is a serial entrepreneur and branding strategist for corporations, celebrities, and everyday individuals who are looking to build and develop their business. Hiring her was quite pricy, but when looking at price, you have to decide if you're going to pay now and learn the right way, or pay later and risk losing everything. Between Syleecia and Tiana, I must say Pen Legacy and Charron Monaye are in the right position. I had a business idea before connecting with them, but I did not have a brand that related me to my target audience. This was the biggest reason why my brand lacked clients. I was failing to connect and speak to the lives of my audience. All I was doing was selling and pitching my books instead of considering:

- Who would be most likely to read my books?
- Who would most likely be interested in the value of my product or service?
- What demographic groups would buy my products?
- When and where would they buy them?
- Would I purchase my own product or service?
- The marketplace and what kinds of books and stories are already being told. You never what to duplicate what is already done, but rather enhance to offer a different result.

Marketing

Now that we have the business set up and brand established, let's briefly talk about marketing. This is where you start investing and promoting your products and services. Even though you are getting a lot of work done, you are still not in a position to quit your job yet. If you completed your business set-up and hired a branding coach to help you implement your business identity, you should be halfway broke by now. That paycheck is almost better than God's grace, isn't it? When I was building, I would pray for Friday to come so I could see money, only to watch it pass through one hand and into another. Some Fridays I felt like I was borrowing my own paycheck and experienced guilt if I spent a dime on myself. But, imagine how life would have been if I did not have consistent paychecks.

Marketing is one of, if not *the most* important part of your business. In a world where entrepreneurship is maturing, the marketplace is saturated with every kind of product, service, and entrepreneur. *Fortune Magazine* (2017) reports that the "Bureau of Labor Statistics (BLS) data showing the number of self-employed people in the U.S. has grown by nearly 150,000 since 2014 to 8,751,000—up from 8,602,000 by the end of 2016. A large majority (85.7%) of these new founders were over 40 years old." So how do you compete? How do you market your business?

Marketing is everything a company does to acquire customers and maintain a relationship with them. Even small tasks, such as writing a thank-you letter, playing golf with a prospective client, returning calls promptly, and meeting with a past or present client for coffee, can be thought of as marketing. The ultimate goal of marketing is to match a company's products and services to the people who need and want them. Just like with branding, there are four P's of marketing that is needed in order to create a successful campaign. They are product, price, place, and promotion.

- **Product** refers to an item or items a business plans to sell. When examining a product, some important questions should be asked. Such as, what differentiates the product from its competitors, can the product be marketed with a secondary product, and are there substitute products in the market?
- **Price** refers to how much the product will cost. When establishing price, consider the unit price to produce or

publish, marketing costs and distribution expenses, and the value of the information/product.

- **Place** refers to how you will distribute the product or service. How will people find it?
- **Promotion** refers to your communications campaign. Promotional activities may include advertising, personal selling, sales promotions, public relations, direct marketing, sponsorship, and guerrilla marketing.

Having an answer to these four P's will enable you to reach a large client base, sell your products or services, and become a competitive entity within your industry. If you are already in business, here are some ways you can improve your marketing for massive results.

Learn from Competitors. When searching for ways to improve your marketing, look to your competitors. Find out what they are doing to attract customers.

Get Testimonials. Before people buy something, they often look for reviews that validate their purchase. People want to know they're spending money on quality. You can put your reviews in multiple places so potential customers are sure to see them. You can add reviews to your website. You might have a dedicated testimonials page, or you might let customers review your products.

Use Social Media. You probably already know that social media marketing is important for small businesses. But, simply having accounts isn't enough. There are always new social media marketing tips for small business that can improve your presence on social platforms.

- First, keep your account information updated and accurate. If something about your business changes, your social media profile should change, too.
- Second, post fresh content. You must regularly post new content on your social media pages. Frequent posts keep you in front of customers' faces. Post about new products and sales, and show your followers what you and your business are up to.

Gain Exposure. Whether you have a storefront or a home-based business, it's important for potential customers to get to know you and your business. Sometimes that means you have to go out to where your customers are instead of waiting for them to come to you.

Become an Expert. You can improve your small business marketing by positioning yourself as a local expert. Becoming an expert is one of the long-term marketing tactics for small business but can provide a big payoff. Find local interest group meetings that fit in with your business's brand. Attend them to network, find customers, and show off your expertise. You can offer yourself as a speaker at local events and meetings. You might also do demonstrations. Leverage the networking benefits of joining a chamber of commerce.

Write Your Business Plan

Do you need a break?

Tired yet?

And you thought you were going to quit today and become wealthy tomorrow. Entrepreneurship is work! Just think about it. I, along with others, have accomplished all of this while working. It may seem like a lot, but I promise you that doing this will elevate you not only as a person, but as a business within the world. Imagine receiving an email from someone in another continent inquiring about doing business with you. Wouldn't that be exciting? I know it was for me. That's why I didn't accept new clients immediately after publishing Summer's book. I needed to make sure Pen Legacy was in alignment with my mission, vision, and values. Getting clear on that made me brainstorm and answer the same questions I am asking you to answer. I had to write out the vision, make it plain, and do my research so everything would be ready for the world to see.

By fall of 2015, I was ready to share this new venture with the world. Because I had adapted my first book My Side of the Story into the play, *Living Your Life*, that premiered in Philadelphia in 2012 and in Washington D.C. at the D.C. Black Theater Festival in 2013, most of my clients wanted to adapt their books into scripts. Then, a co-worker by the name of Vaughn McNeill asked me to publish his book, *Respect Your Choices: Finding Balance in Success.*

Pen Legacy was open and ready for business, but I still had to face my biggest challenge ever – pricing. I could not digest charging the "real" prices for my services out of fear of losing clients or having no clients. So, I undercharged most of the time, which left me having to pay the balances for them. I walked away in the *red* majority of the time and in credit card debt all of the time.

1st Lesson Learned:

You must price to cover all expenses. Because I priced so low, I paid the difference between the revenue and expense to help people's dreams come true. Proper pricing is the difference between you elevating your business and bankrupting yourself. One of my author friends used to tell me, "*Your prices are non-negotiable. Never compromise your business or yourself to make things reasonable for people. People will pay for what they want, and if they want your services or product, they will find the money.*" And she would end every conversation with, "*People respect your business and time when they have to pay for it.*" After hearing that enough, I thought, *She's right. Why should I discount myself to make it "easier" for others to afford me, only to lose financially and not have my time respected?* So, price changes were implemented, and the day of easy was over.

2nd Lesson Learned:

Never let people dictate your prices. Sure, you can offer sales to move inventory, but everyday should not be a markdown. How will you ever grow your business doing this? Sometimes, your price tag can draw your target clients to you. In other words, if you price right, your business will build right.

Ultimately, you have to find other ways to gain capital for your business. I don't mean using credit cards and taking out business loans. I am an avid watcher of the show *Shark Tank*, and I am always taking notes from Barbara Corcoran, Mark Cuban, and Daymond John. Kevin O'Leary is tough, but listening to his criticism and questions makes me evaluate my business even more. They teach you what investors look for, what you should be zoning in on, and help you to identify if your business is truly a business, brand or a hobby. I provided you with a lot of the questions the *Shark Tank* casts ask, minus inquiries regarding the total number of sales and revenue earned. Good thing is, if you ever consider going on *Shark Tank* or in front of an investor, you'll be prepared.

Many of these questions and figuring out how to strategize your business can be found in a document called a business plan. A business plan is essentially your answers to a comprehensive list of questions that will show your road to success. It will also indicate to an investor the current need and potential growth of your business. A business plan structure looks something like this:

Business Plan

1.   **Executive Summary**: Why is your business uniquely qualified to succeed?

2.   **Company Analysis**: What products and/or services do you offer now and/or what will you develop and offer in the future?

3.   **Industry Analysis**: How big is/are your market(s) and how are they changing? What trends are affecting them and do these trends bode well for your future success?

4.   **Competitive Analysis:** Who are your competitors and what are each of their key strengths and weaknesses? In what areas will you have or gain competitive advantage? How?

5.   **Customer Analysis**: Who are your target customers? What are their demographic and/or psychographic profiles? What are their needs?

6.   **Marketing Plan**: How will you reach your target customers? What promotional tactics and marketing channels will you use? How will you price your products and/or services? What brand positioning do you desire for each?

7.   **Management Team**: Who comprises your current team and what key hires must you make in order to execute on the opportunity in front of you. Will you build a Board of Advisors or Directors, and if so, who will the email you you seek?

8.   **Operations Plan**: What is your action plan? What are the milestones you must accomplish to go from where you are now to where you want to be at year's end? How about at the end of five years?

9.   **Financial Plan**: How much external funding (if applicable) do you need to build your company? In what areas will these funds be invested? What are your projected revenues and profits over the next one to five years? What assets must you acquire?

As I'm sure you noticed, we already answered a lot of these questions, so completing a business plan should be quite easy. Some sections you will have to forecast based on your pricing and expenses. The growth of your business depends on your revenue intake. If you show more expenses than revenue, there is evidence that your business will not flourish, thus causing no investor to work with you. You see, investors will work with small business owners who show potential, but to show no growth is a big no-no. Also, keep in mind that an investor's money is nothing more than a loan. They are giving you money, with interest, and requesting a stake in your company. So, ask yourself, *Am I ready to give up control of my company and a percentage of my earnings for success*? If you answered no, keep working and use a business plan as your guide to get on track. My business plan helped me go from a company whose "books" were always in the red to a company who, in 2017, earned a profit and therefore has to start paying taxes.

Did you catch that?

I started writing in 2009 and launched my business in 2014, but in 2017 I'm finally seeing a profit and have to file taxes in 2018. After nine years of writing, building, grinding, and learning, I finally closed a year on top! This is what I want for you, but prayfully, you'll be able to accomplish it in less time. But, no matter how long it takes you, as long as you do it right, your results will mirror that of success.

Choose a Business Structure

In 2017, I had to form a business structure for my business because I was generating *profits* that were deemed taxable income. So, because I am afraid of going to prison for tax invasion, I formed a limited liability company to add liable protection against my personal assets and prepare the business to now file taxes. Uncle Sam is always watching and waiting for you to excel so he can take his percentage. After reading and studying under financial guru Dave Ramsey, I learned about business finances and taxes. In addition, my accountant Khristina Barnes of KMB Tax Services prompted me that it was time. One of the things I read from Dave's blogs was:

"Legally, if you make over $600 gross income on the business in one quarter, then you're supposed to file quarterly estimates on your taxes and pay withholding. And that should usually come out to around 25%. So, for instance, if you make $10,000 and spend $9,000, then you have $1,000 left to take home. Write a check for $750 to yourself and a check for $250 to go into your tax savings account. That will take care of your taxes. But, this percentage can change depending on the type of business structure you have."

With my LLC structure, I started setting aside one-fourth of any profits earned per quarter in a small business account for taxes. Doing this has saved me from worrying if I'll have the money readily available when it comes time to owing the IRS.

If you are not sure which structure would be beneficial for you, contact a business or tax professional who handles this kind of work. Your business structure determines which income tax form you have to file and the organization of your business, i.e. board members, stakeholders, etc. The most common structures of business are:

o Sole Proprietorship
o Partnership
o Corporation
o S Corporation
o Limited Liability Company (LLC)

Now let's look at each one of them individually so you know what structure is suitable for your business.

Sole Proprietorship ~ With a sole proprietorship, someone owns an unincorporated business by himself or herself. However, if you are the sole member of a domestic limited liability company (LLC), you are not a sole proprietor if you elect to treat the LLC as a corporation.

Partnership ~ A partnership is the relationship existing between two or more persons who join to carry on a trade or business. Each person contributes money, property, labor or skill, and expects to share in the profits and losses of the business.

Corporation ~ In forming a corporation, prospective shareholders exchange money, property, or both, for the corporation's capital stock. A corporation generally takes the same deductions as a sole proprietorship to figure its taxable income. A corporation can also take special deductions. For federal income tax purposes, a C corporation is recognized as a separate taxpaying entity. A corporation conducts business, realizes net income or loss, pays taxes, and distributes profits to shareholders.

S Corporation ~ S corporations are corporations that elect to pass corporate income, losses, deductions, and credits through to their shareholders for federal tax purposes.

Limited Liability Company (LLC) ~ A Limited Liability Company (LLC) is a business structure allowed by state statute. Each state may use different regulations, so you should check with your state if you are interested in starting a Limited Liability Company. Owners of an LLC are called members. Most states do not restrict ownership, and so members may include individuals, corporations, other LLCs, and foreign entities. There is no maximum number of members. Most states also permit single-member LLCs, those having only one owner.

If you've studied the marketplace, you will notice that a lot of small businesses use the Limited Liability Corporation structure simply because being an LLC provides their member's protection from liability. This means members are not personally liable for debts and court judgments incurred by the LLC. Creditors are foreclosed from seeking the personal assets of the LLC's members. It is a meaningful shield not provided in a sole proprietorship or traditional partnership.

Pitching Your Business

This is the moment you've waited for!

You've laid a solid foundation by knowing your why, making your business official, creating your marketing plans, and working out the logistics. Now it's time to tell the world about your business! Between your website, social media, and logos, it's time for you to introduce yourself and pitch your business. This is where you generate conversation, create buzz, connect to your potential customers, share your story, and build your network.

3rd Lesson Learned:

People buy from people who they connect with, like, and trust. People don't always purchase or support your business because they really want to try what you offer or read what you wrote. They purchase from you because they support who are and what you are doing in the world. I have loyal supporters who have every book I ever released, and to this day, they have never read any of them. Connect! Connect! Connect!

I know many of you are saying, "I suck at pitching or selling my business," and that's okay. I *HATE* pitching, too. However, in the world of entrepreneurship, pitching is how you get clients, investors, and attract others. Look at it this way, pitching is just like having a conversation. You talk about who you are and things you have to offer. Now, in order for this to flow correctly, you have to know who you are and who to talk to. Moreover, having great energy about yourself and your business will help you connect to a person even if your pitch is not the greatest. I have seen people connect solely based on energy vibes alone.

Remember, you have what they want. Your business is aimed to solving a problem. Therefore, you should leverage that and connect the dots to create the perfect masterpiece on why they should invest, support, or partner with you! There are four components, in my opinion, that your pitch needs to include:

- **What's in it for them?**
- **Be concrete.**

- **Be unapologetically disruptive.**
- **Prove that growth is sustainable.**

Going back to *Shark Tank*, you will notice that each shark wants to see how they can gain something from investing. Some will actually see past the "lack of" sales and focus on the potential and energy. Other sharks will listen to their back story and engage because they, too, had a similar experience. Through the many times I've pitch, I have found that if you pitch your business as *solving the problem*, rather than *selling the product*, you have a better chance of winning.

Last thing before I close out this chapter. When it comes to pitching, DO NOT let the word "No" discourage you. "No" is a word that most entrepreneurs use to motivate them. I have turned every "No" I've received since 2009 into a revenue stream for myself or used it as a platform to soar on. One thing about true entrepreneurs is that we are creative and do not let naysayers stop us. If someone denies you, don't stop. Learn, network, and create your own. I could not get a major publishing deal with a traditional company because it was said "poetry is too hard to market and not sellable." So, I went through a small press company to gain exposure and then created my own. Accepting "No" also works in your personal life, because if you are like me, you will hear it there, too. That's the cool thing I enjoy about being an entrepreneur. A lot of the strategies and things you need to build a successful business can be transferred to build a rewarding and stress-free life.

"I Want to Quit My Job"
Entrepreneurial Conversation...

Nikia Hannon has been an educator for over twenty years. She received her Bachelors in English, Secondary Education from Millersville University in 1996 and her Masters in Educational Leadership at Widener University in 2002. Nikia served as an English teacher on both the middle and high school levels for seven years and as part of the administrative team at the middle and high school and district office levels for thirteenyears. Currently, Nikia is the proud owner of the ND Hannon Group, which provides instructional services to families, teachers, and students in Wilmington, Delaware, and the surrounding areas.

Nikia is a member of Zeta Phi Beta Sorority, Inc. She attended the Harvard Leadership Institute for Urban Leadership in the summer of 2012. She worked with the Gloucester County Minority Coalition on their Scholarship Step Show at Kingsway Regional High School from 2004-2007. She has received certificates of appreciation for her work with both G.R.A.C.E and U.P.L.I.F.T. mentoring programs.

Nikia is extremely excited that God has blessed her to marry her best friend, Kenneth Hannon. "And we know that all things work together for good to them that love God, to them who are the called according to his purpose." To God Be the Glory!

Contact Info:
Email: Nhannon@hope4schools.com
Phone: 302-285-9749
Website: www.hope4schools.com

As an educator, you have done a lot of work with our youth. Please tell us about your prior work and why you created ND Hannon Group?

In August 1997, I began my lifelong passion of mentoring youth. I started with a core group of fifteen students in my middle school, focusing on basic time management, conflict resolution, and improving self-image. In May 2000, I expanded my mentoring program and partnered with mysorority to form the award-winning mentoring program U.P.L.I.F.T – Utilizing Potential Life Interests for Teens. Over the past thirteen years, the program has assisted hundreds of young women with time management, money management, proper etiquette, and many more areas of achievement. Most recently I formed G.R.A.C.E – Girls Reaching Academic and Cultural Excellence at Christiana High School. The purpose of G.R.A.C.E is to change the lives of at-risk young ladies and give them the proper tools to end the cycle of continuous out-of-school suspensions, boost their academic success rates, and increase their attendance rates. The overall goal is to change their behavioral patterns so they will graduate in a timely manner. I currently have a 100% success rate for these young ladies.

After seeing the growth and results of the mentoring groups, I took my passion for education to the next level and gave birth to ND Hannon Group. Wanting to help bridge the educational gap and increase overall capacity in our educational facilities, I partnered with several schools in the area, institutions of higher learning, and a national non-profit organization to make our students globally competitive. I work with teachers on best practices, run a tutoring program that focuses on individualized growth for students, and assists young entrepreneurs building their dreams of financial freedom.

As an entrepreneur, what are some of the challenges you face? What strategies have you mastered in order to stay in business?

There are so many challenges with being an entrepreneur, but my biggest was going from being a part of a team to being by myself. I am a one-man band, so every aspect of my business from payroll, to licensing, to marketing and advertising, to contractor questions, to client complaints, to parent concerns - it all comes through me. What helps is being passionate about your business. I love providing educational services to families and schools.So with that, the challenges are just part of your everyday life.

As far as mastery, I honestly haven't found what I have mastered yet; I am still learning! There are new surprises daily, which forces me to revisit my business plan or my advertising scheme. I will say I've gotten better with time management and budgeting.

How did you financially prepare yourself prior to leaving your employer in order to pursue your business full-time?

I "fired" my boss twice; the first time was a disaster. My company was hired to provide services to a school for a year. The contract was standard and made no provisions in case of an emergency. I created a three-year budget based on the projected profits and promptly resigned from my current position. Because I used this contract with the client previously, it didn't dawn on me to hire a lawyer. Two months into the project, the client went broke and cancelled the contract. With no contingency plan and no money for a lawyer, I was forced to take the hit and work odd jobs attempting to recover. Unfortunately, I had to return to a full-time job. The second time I made sure I had enough cash flow for the next three years and a new series of signed contracts with contingencies added to protect my company before firing my boss.

Knowing what you know now about entrepreneurship, what are three things you would have done differently before resigning from your job? And why?

- ✓ I would ensure that my contracts had contingency plans in case of emergencies so I can be compensated in some form for them breaking the contract.
- ✓ Along those lines, I would have had a lawyer on retainer from the beginning to help protect my business.
- ✓ I would have garnered a creative team and a project manager from the beginning to assist me in growing my business.

What resources have you used to get financial support and investments?

Because I am in educational support, there aren't a lot (to my knowledge) of places to get financial support. I visited my state representative who oversees Small Business Development and went to several small business workshops, but none assisted me with funding. I did attend a grant-writing workshop, which helped with understanding how to gain funds in the future.

Being a woman who wears many titles, how do you find time to balance life, love, and entrepreneurship?

My husband and family support my passion and encourage me at all times with my business. At first, it wasn't easy when I had meetings at all hours and on weekends, but now it is part of our routine. I do make time for just family. My clients and service providers know Sundays is off limits to business. Also, I do not answer emails or calls when I take vacation time. My business follows my career path, so it isn't a far stretch from my life as an administrator.

What advice would you offer to someone who is thinking about resigning from their employer tomorrow to invest their time into their business?

Set boundaries for yourself. The more access people have to you, the harder it will be to have that life balance you are seeking. When I first started, I was up all hours of the night and I loved it, but I did not allow others to invade those crazy hours. When I was "off", I stayed off. I only answered the phone or emails in emergency situations. Once people know they have access to you, you will lose that time for yourself. Don't be afraid to aim high! Nothing is out of reach with prayer and commitment. Lastly, do not go for the quick money; it won't last and you will burn out quickly. Follow your passion! Work is only work when you've lost the love for what you do!

Strategy #3
Remaining Committed to the Goal

"*Commitment means staying loyal to what you said you were going to do long after the mood you said it in has left you.*" This is one of the realest quotes I have read as it compares to entrepreneurship. Understanding that entrepreneurship can be a risk and securing potential clients are a gamble, you have to either believe in the vision and/or pursue something you love. This is why you consistently hear people say, "Make sure you are doing something you love", because depending on the public to support and elevate your dreams is unbearable for many. I have seen a lot of people close up shop because they lacked clients and their business were not generating money.

There have been many times when my commitment to my company, Pen Legacy, LLC, wavered and my desire to just return to the workforce and be normal seemed to be a better choice. But then, I was quickly reminded why I embarked on this journey in the first place and all that I have managed to achieve. I visualize my clients' excitement when they receive their books, sometimes personally delivered by me, and they get to hold their dream in their hands for the first time. As an author, it is no greater feeling in the world than to see your hard work materialized and your story released. So, instead of quitting, I get some tea, turn my phone off, and watch Kevin Hart's stand-up comedy shows.

Clearly, everybody is not like me. So, in this chapter, I will offer ways in which I remained committed even when I didn't see results, have clients, or know when to expect things to start happening. Outside of envisioning great moments, patience, readiness, faith, flexibility, and an amazing support network is why I am still standing years later.

Patience

Out of everything I have used to remain committed to this journey, patience has kept me sane and not wanting to flip tables or catch a case. I am here to tell you, entrepreneurship, lack of money, and clients' attitudes will make you question your whole life. But, over the years, I had to find ways to be more understanding and available, even when I was mentally spent. I had to understand that what I envisioned was not going to happen overnight. Some people might have you thinking if you quit your job today to write a book or start a business, you will be successful tomorrow. If it were that easy, you would see more millionaires. We would not need shows like *Shark Tank*, and we would be replacing coaches with tax and financial experts. Since that is not the case, we have to develop a sense of "wait". The good thing about waiting is you can use the downtime to prepare, network, and personally grow as a person.

This way, when opportunity hits, you are mentally prepared for the journey and ready to go.

Readiness

I often tell my coaching clients that their personal life is a reflection of their business. If your personal credit is not good, your business credit won't be either. If you have an attitude problem in your personal life, you will lack clients and receive alot of complaints in your business. So, there is a lot of personal work we could be doing during this "wait" time. This is also important because you are ultimately the BRAND! People decide if and how they will support you based on who you are and the lifestyle you show. In these times of social media and technology, people will research you before they invest in you.

Why?

Because they want to make sure the person (or company) is who they are selling themselves to be. I know many entrepreneurs who are not living the life they are selling, and someone with my mindset, I often wonder how is that possible. For example, they are building a company that promises to get you out of debt, but they are always crying on social media about trying to get out of debt. *"Is what you're selling not working?"* I always ask. In my opinion, you are the first consumer or client of your business. Your company's first win should start with you so you can use that testimonial to pitch.

Before I started Pen Legacy and was just a writer, my life was a mess. I was making money but still broke. I was lying to myself, pretending to be successful when I was not. You know how we think we are motivating ourselves, but all we're really doing is blowing smoke because what we *think* is more important than what we *see*. Yeah, that was me, until a co-worker saw past my façade and challenged me on my perception. It was almost like he was in my mind everyday. Even though I talked a good game, nothing, and I mean *nothing*, in my life mirrored what I spoke. When the time came and I announced that I had a business, his only reply was, "So." Hearing his nonchalant response hurt me to my core, and analyzing it made me realize I was not what I was promoting. In all honesty, nothing in my life was empowering.

I was miserable.

I was self-sabotaging myself to keep me where people thought I should be.

I had bad credit and no money.

I had no real author success.

I was busy doing everything but really accomplished nothing. In 2013, that was me! On social media, I was well put together, but in real life, I was broken, busted, and disgusted. I was getting shut-off notices, dodging bill collectors, and praying for God to make my days brighter. But, when you talked to me, I gave the impression that everything was great. Charron had no problems! Entrepreneurship was awesome. HA! Entrepreneurship was great, but my mess became the poison that would soon make me decide between my image and my business. As a result, I had to step back and correct myself because I thought, *If he saw the real me, then who else sees it?*

Moreover, the house where I was living at the time was actually being rented to me incorrectly, and along with some other things, I was told I had to move out. I moved into the house on November 30th, and after making this house a home, I was told to move out June 3rd of the following year. I had no savings and bad credit. Where would I move to? Was this my punishment for not being authentically honest? Whatever the reason, I was being tested and tried seriously.

With my mother's support, my kids and I were told we could move into my aunt Margaret's house in Roslyn, Pennsylvania. With this second chance and better opportunity, I vowed to the Lord to get myself together. So, in the midst of dealing with my hurt, betrayal, insecurity, irresponsible financial management, and being a people pleaser, I wrote a book about my journey to rediscovering myself. When I released *Love the Real You*, the way I saw myself and my business changed.

Lesson Learned #1: Always be who you are no matter what. Everybody will have their opinion about you and others will create reasons why they don't like you, but remain true to you.

Lesson Learned #2: Financial management is key to a healthy life and business. When I received that call saying I had to move, having no money or credit, it felt like a death wish. Not only was I not living honestly, I was broke while claiming to be successful.

My transparency in *Love the Real You* made it my biggest selling book thus far in my career. It also awarded me the #1 spot on Amazon.com in the Spiritual Healing category. Celebrities posed with the book and shared it to their networks, which not only brought me more sells, but the exposure that I was always looking to receive. Plus, my book landed on the shelves in Barnes & Noble next to Steve Harvey's book. See what happens when you get yourself together. I accepted my foolishness, gained clarity, did the work, and walked away with a testimony of a second chance to be me.

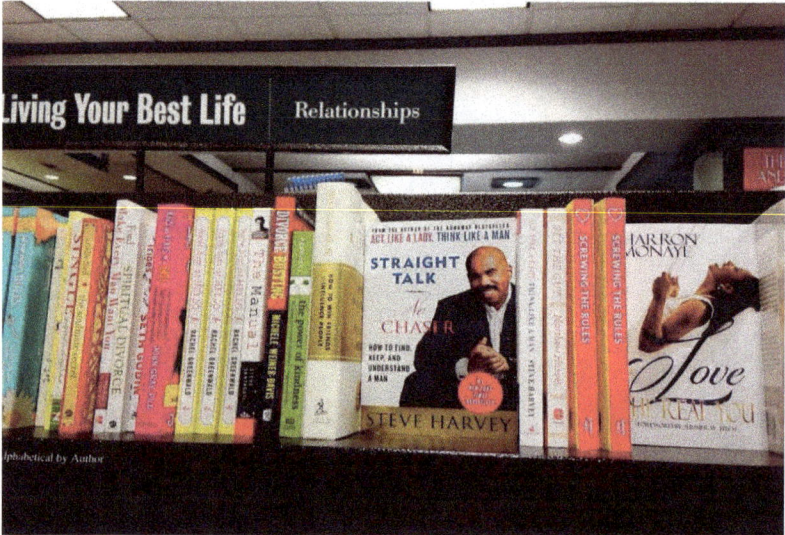

Now that I live and serve in my truth, with my own voice, and remain committed to myself, my business has evolved. It was like God was waiting for me to walk into His image of me before He could bless me. Have you experienced that? What you prayed for happens, and what you need comes before you can even ask.

Love the Real You was released in May of 2015, and after that, I took my next jump and became committed to helping others reach their potential. God did not save and bless me for me to keep it to myself. I had a story to tell, and in telling mine, I had people willing to share their own! To God be the glory, they hired my company to help them write their story in either book form or for the stage!

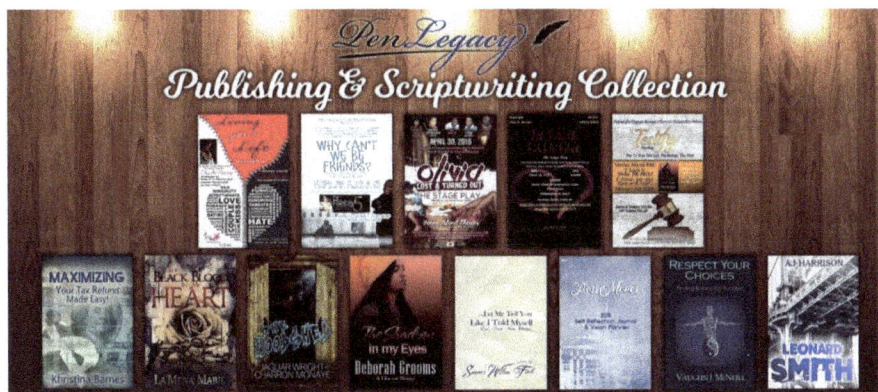

So, as you see, I had to personally get ready for what I wanted so God could bless me with the opportunity to serve and further build this company. Are you ready for business? Are you in a position to run a business? You will never be blessed with what you want if you do not show that you can handle it!

Faith

If it had not been for the Lord on my side, where would I be? Have you noticed whenever someone accepts an award, gets honored, gives a speech, or talks about how they've overcome something, they speak of their way maker? Regardless of *who* you believe in, you know there is a greater power that protects, blesses, and provides all of your needs. Knowing this gives you the comfort to keep pushing through. In my opinion, faith makes commitment easy, especially if you know that with continued hard work, honesty, and love it will happen. I'm not saying you have to be holier than the pope. However, with prayer, fasting, and sometimes just sitting still while waiting for a sign or clarity to move forward, it will save you from making mistakes that could hurt you.

Before I really allowed God to be the leader in my life, I moved on impulse instead of alignment, would blame myself if something didn't work out, and looked at rejection as failure for not being who they wanted me to be. However, when I gave my life and my business to the Lord, He gave me the ability to see what was in front of me, the gift to differentiate between foolishness and opportunity, and the wisdom to know that any rejection given was His protection over me. I started to look at myself differently. The one thing I know for sure is who Charron is, and I am here to say that the life I'm presently living is one I always dreamed of. After doing hard work on myself, realigning my business, removing the dead weight, and working with the expectation of money coming to me, there isn't much that I long to have. I am still waiting for that amazing man to marry me, but I know that's coming, too.

Flexibility

As an entrepreneur, you MUST be flexible and acceptable to change. No matter what product you sell or service you offer, it must be relevant and trending. There are people who refuse to change the way they do things or add products to leverage their business because it's not true to their mission. I understand the whole "mission and vision" concept, but not adapting to our society's economic and technology trends will only lead to an early closing of your business.

Entrepreneurship is no different than any other business, including clothing lines, music trends, or filmology. Everything evolves over time. For example, today's fashion is not the same as it was in the 70's or 80's. Back in the 70's, people wore bell bottoms, big collared shirts, platform shoes, and jumpsuits. Today's trends seem to be skinny jeans, crop tops, and backless shirts. Even the hairstyles are different. We went from rocking Afros to wearing weaves! So, if things around you are changing, how do you think your business can grow remaining the same? This is why knowing your industry and remaining educated on the trends is important to you staying relevant.

Supportive Network

Having a supportive network as an entrepreneur is key. It's also the anchor to your business growing and developing. But, this can be one of the hardest things to come by. Why? Because either people are afraid you'll surpass them or they are not really cheering for your success. In addition, some people can't support you in public because of how they disrespected you behind closed doors. So, finding genuine people with no hidden motives to support you is the hardest task you will have during this journey. And that's just for the entrepreneur side. We're not going to talk about the support of employees, because you already know coworkers and bitter supervisors will set you up and throw you all the way under the bus. The bright side, though, is there are people out there who believe in you. You just have to connect with them, but remember to be honest in your approach and request.

Throughout my journey, I have run across some people who supported me for free, while others attached a price tag to their support. However, no one has supported me through this journey more than my children and mother. It was my mother who saw the potential in my writing; she told me at the age of fourteen that writing was my gift after hearing me recite my poem, "Alone", at a UNCF telethon banquet. When I decided to go to Atlanta to meet Kandi and then fly to Los Angeles for the songwriter's conference, she gave her blessing. She has every book I've ever written, been to every play, and listened to every complaint I had about this business. At times, she was mom, girlfriend, counselor, and babysitter. What amazed me the most was that she wasn't always 100% sold on a lot of my moves. Still, even with her questions and concerns, she never said "STOP" or told me to give up. And for that I am so grateful! Even when I wanted to quit, she motivated me to keep pushing. That kind of support was my cushion to bounce back after every fall. Along with her, I have my children, Chris and Craig. Now Chris, my oldest, grew up in this business. He was six years old when I started this journey and went to a majority of the book signings, literary events, and conferences that I attended. He was there passing out my flyers, showing people my books, and telling everyone who would listen just how great I was. We sold out of books at some signings that we did simply because he was pitching like his life depended on it. Even though it didn't, he knew how disappointed I would be if I had to take any boxes of books back home with us.

Chris is my biggest cheerleader. Whether I win or fail, he wipes the tears before they fall and helps me deposits checks when they come. That's why it only made sense for me to make him co-owner of Pen Legacy when it came time to legalize the business. At first, I didn't think he would want the title because of all the struggling and headaches he saw me endure while trying to run it, but when I asked him, he said *YES* without any hesitation. His acceptance made my dream even more important, because not only did I want to create a business, I wanted my stories and my business to be my legacy. Knowing my son will keep my legacy alive even after I'm gone makes me hustle that much harder to elevate and become even more successful. I don't feel it is good enough to leave him just a "business". I'm motivated to leave him a *successful* business that will work even when he does not feel like it!

In addition to the support I receive from my mother and children, I have the support of friends, Facebook friends who I have never met, and of course, my coaches. My work ethic and seriousness about this entrepreneur journey has made people recognize my business and extend a helping hand. Facebook is where I've found my biggest support. No, not every supporter will buy my products or services, but the nature of my needs is not always monetary. For example, I was blessed to connect with Lucinda Cross, the Chief Activator and visionary behind the vision boards. She was on the show *Queen Boss*, which came on Centic (now BetHer), and she is the founder of the Activate brand. When I connected with her, our work ethic and girl power made us support each other. Whenever she asked for my help, I gave with no questions asked, and she did likewise. In 2016, she penned the foreword for my fourth book, *STOP Asking for Permission and Give Notice*. When she dropped her vision board kits, I purchased some for my entrepreneur coaching group. Remind you, this connection was established in 2015, and I just had the opportunity to meet her in person in 2017 at her final Activate Conference in New York.

So how do you gain support for your business? These are some tips that have been helpful for me:

Focus on the right people. Some people mess up by trying to connect to everyone. They attend every event, take everyone's business cards, and befriend anybody on social media. Then they're not sure who is who and how to leverage the connection. One of the things I do before connecting with anyone is do a Google search on them to find out who they are and how we can help each other. You have to know who you are meeting. Meeting people just for the sake of it is not good business practice. However, when you do your homework first and have a plan in place, you can make that initial conversation more meaningful, which can lead to a possible follow-up.

Create win-win situations. In my last example, I said I do a Google search on them to find out who they are and how we can help each other. Never seek out a support person or network where you are the only person winning. When it comes to any relationship in life, whether business or personal, there must be give and take, but everyone must win in the end. It will be hard to find someone who is waiting to willingly hand over their contacts and information to you that helped make them successful just so you can win. No! What's in it for them? You will get more when you both shine, rather than you stealing their light to shine alone.

Be clear on your supportneeds. The most ineffective thing you can do when building support is not knowing what you need. I totally dislike when people come to me for help but don't know what they need help with, and then get upset with me because I am not a mind reader. Nobody—unless they are a coach, and even that is questionable—can help you get clear on anything if you don't know the initial direction or mission. Before asking for help, have your plan in place.

Use social networks. For me, social media has been a lifesaver. Between the connections I've made and the groups that I belong to, there is always someone genuine that can offer support. You can ask a question in a group and get fifty answers. Not only did they make it easy for you, but they gave you practices that they know work. In my opinion, experience and life lessons are the best teachers. I do not like taking advice that has not been tried or tested. By people sharing their wins and losses along with their advice, I can decide which way will be best for me. Some advice has saved me a ton of money, as well. Looking back, I must say that I have spent enough.

Don't be too busy that you don't attend networking events. I don't know what makes people think they are so good at what they do that they don't have to socialize, network, or connect with people. I know you live a crazy life, whether married with kids or broke and alone, but if no one knows you, how can they support you? Have you ever heard the saying, "It's not what you know, but who you know"? Networking can be the difference between you getting an opportunity from someone that otherwise wouldn't have given you the time of day and someone walking past you at an event and ignoring your advances. Being an entrepreneur, networking is how you advance in your career. It's the same being an employee. If you come to work every day and just do your job, don't socialize, and leave at your end time and not a minute later, do you think your boss will mention your name when the director solicits for someone to promote or lead a project? Again, entrepreneur and employee status mirror each other a lot, and your success in either depends on how much you are willing to get out there. Nobody will support you if they don't know you.

Volunteer. You will be surprised how much support you can gain by volunteering your time and services for the betterment of your community and society. You have to know when to give back. Service is big when it comes to finding support and being supported. Having a successful business is not enough! Nobody cares that you are the founder of a profitable business if you aren't giving back in some way. If you noticed, a majority of millionaires and billionaires donate their time and money to many humanitarian efforts. They don't sit on social media bragging and boasting about #WINNING. They win, then reach back and help others win. They partner with other organizations so that the less fortunate can be fortunate! Being a selfish entrepreneur will only keep you searching for help instead of being the help others seek.

Strategy #4:
Your Employer is your First Investor, Capitalize On It!

Your job is your first investor for your business. Did you know that? Some will settle for business loans and others will look to family and friends for funding, but did you know your employer is the best investor yet?

The money is paid on time.

There is no interest accruing.

You can work overtime to earn more.

Taxes are already being taken out.

So, even though we are working to resign to fulfill our dream full-time, our jobs are important as we build our business and strategize our exit. When you think of your job, you go there for eight to twelve hours a day, and in return, they provide you with:

Steady Income

Since starting with the Department of Veteran Affairs, I've gotten one promotion, jumped three grades, and elevated pay steps that corresponded with pay increases. I am paid faithfully bi-weekly no matter what happens. My paycheck is never late, and it's not contingent upon someone paying the VA so they can pay me. Every other Friday my paycheck is deposited into my account. This steady income gives me the ability to properly plan my business, personal life, and travel. My net income never decreases, and they don't piece meal my paycheck to me. I render a service, and they pay me accordingly. This is essential to anybody, but it makes life doable when you are waiting to be paid from clients in your business. Knowing I have a steady income gives me the ability to still live life with little worry while creating my business with ease.

Experience

At my current job, I am a Senior Claims Examiner. I process disability and death claims for veterans and their dependents. I am the decision maker between if a veteran will be able to purchase his medication or not, but in accordance with the laws and regulations set by Congress and the Pension and Fiduciary Services in Washington, D.C. My job can be extremely stressful and exhausting because of the demands of our leadership and management; however, my job has given me transferable skills that I now implement in my business. My position also requires me to be very detail-orientated and understand legal regulations. Overlooking the minutest detail on a claim can result in a veteran losing their benefits or becoming homeless. Overlooking the minutest detail on a contract for Pen Legacy can result in me being sued.

An Opportunity to Build Your Network

My job allows me to build connections with more people and expand my"influential" rolodex. I am always surprised by the caliber of people I meet working across the government. I have met other entrepreneurs, potential investors, social connections, and clients who not only have published under my company, but now have a vested interest and refer my business to everyone who needs writing services.

Learning Time Management

Having only a limited amount of time daily to devote to my business forced me to become extremely diligent about keeping on top of my calendar, daily task execution, and managing my time. Having three hours after work and eight hours on the weekends meant I was only able to focus on those things that were most important in moving my venture forward while keeping everything extremely streamlined.

In my opinion, my business is where it is today financially and structure-wise because of my paychecks from the Department of Veteran Affairs. The consistent income, opportunity for overtime, annual raises, and promotions all contributed to the financial backing to Charron Monaye "The

Author" and Pen Legacy "The Company". If I did not have this income and was forced to find capital from an investor, I would still be grinding and checking off things to do to get my business off the ground. Even though I started my business in 2009, I did not get clear on my personal direction as a writer or my company ideas as a business owner until 2016. Yes, you read that right.

If you remember back in the entrepreneurial chapter, I mentioned I've been jumping since 2009, taste testing everything as a writer and entrepreneur. One thing I must say, I have been constant as a writer, from writing books, to scripts, to articles, to songwriting. Even in all of that, I spent more money to have the opportunities than I was actually compensated. Do you want to know why? Because it's this thing called *"pay to play"* or *"paying your dues"*. You have to prove your loyalty and commitment to yourself before others invest in you. So, every opportunity I was a part of, I had to either pay to join or fly to get there.

I remember back in 2010 when I was pursuing my songwriting dreams. (This was jump #2). There was a songwriting conference in Los Angeles. I was working with the Department of Veteran Affairs, but I was not yet being compensated well. So, any withdraw of funds from my bank account had to be used for something promising. Seeing this opportunity, I knew I would get the exposure and make the connections needed to get my lyrics heard. So, I paid five hundred dollars to register, and using my next paycheck, I bought my airline ticket and booked the hotel. By the time I flew there on a Wednesday, I had about a dollar and some change in my pocket and no money in my bank account. The great thing was that I was getting paid that coming Friday, but until then, I survived off of water and the pastries at the conference.

The conference was amazing, and I was able to meet and connect with music executives, tour Los Angeles, and for the first time, taste my dream and actually feel that it was obtainable. Being broke did not bother me as much because I knew I had a check coming. When Friday came, though, I ate everything I saw and could buy. Now let's imagine if I was not guaranteed a paycheck that Friday. Do you think I would have gone?

The multiple sacrifices I endured to "pay to play" and "pay my dues" didn't pay off all the time. There were many more expenses where I had to:

- Pay to gain knowledge.
- Pay to gain assistance.
- Pay to travel to an event.
- Pay the expenses to self-publish my books.
- Pay for coaching.
- Pay the studio time and artist to reference my tracks.

In addition, I paid the start-up cost and expenses related to branding my business. You haven't yet heard me say I was paid anything. If I had to estimate how much money I have spent from 2009 to 2016, I would easily say almost a hundred thousand dollars. Even though I have a lot to show for it, I do not have the money to show a profit. But, that all changed in

2017, because I can say I have finally earned *MASSIVE RESULTS AND PROFITS* from my brand as a writer and business owner.

Now I know you must be asking, *What took you so long?* Well, I did not have what I am teaching and sharing with you. I did not have coaches. I could not afford them when I first started. To be very transparent, I didn't really have the money to embark on this entrepreneurial venture. My belief was bigger than my wallet, but I knew if I worked hard, it would one day pay off. If I had the money and mentors to tell me to stop jumping and get focused on one thing, I probably would have saved myself a couple thousands of dollars. But, with me regretting nothing, the jumping created an intensive résumé and gives me the leverage to pitch, write business plans, and create business ventures in any writing capacity because I already have the experience. In addition, being a mother first, I am extremely cautious about my decisions. I never wanted my children to say they went without because of their mommy's dream. So, as much as I spent, I still did not go overboard right away, which caused me to travel at a slower pace, learning as I failed and failing forward. With all of that being said, let's discuss why maintaining your job is necessary.

I completely understand that working as both an employee and an entrepreneur can be a major strain and sacrifice, but as you can see, it can be done. Here are a few strategies to making money and pursuing your dream at the same time:

Consider your job in the right light. No matter what kind of job you have, make sure you consider it a blessing, not a curse. It isn't holding you back; it's keeping you afloat. You need that paycheck. Otherwise, you wouldn't have enough money to live on while you get things going. You're lucky because capital from your current job is available to you every couple of weeks. Most investors want to see that entrepreneurs are investing in themselves first.

Plan your days well. It might sound impressive when someone works 36 hours straight, but you're definitely not managing your time or maintaining your health with that approach. Actually, few businesses are built on that strategy. It's the little, consistent, daily things you do that make or break a startup. Stop the busy work and learn to delegate.

Maximize your time. You have the same hours in each day as Oprah, Tyler Perry, and any other entrepreneur. There are 168 hours in a week to do with as you wish beyond your 40 hours of work, so spend them well. Successful entrepreneurs manage their time; they don't wish for more of it.

See your job as motivation. The more necessary your need is to perform as an entrepreneur, the better you'll do. Find "fuel" to pursue your venture. Always remind yourself that your job is preparing you for your legacy. Trouble doesn't last always.

Outsource. You know what your time is worth. Could you hire someone to do it better, faster, and ultimately break even or make more money by delegating some tasks to others? If so, do it. If you can't afford to hire anyone, have your children, spouse, or friends help you with some of the work you need done. This is where team building and maximizing your resources comes into play. Now I plan my weeks by working five days a week for the Department of Veteran Affairs, three hours a day for Pen Legacy, and allotting myself two weekends a month to spend with my children and loved ones.

"I Want to Quit My Job"
Entrepreneurial Conversation...

Nesi Ewing is a Total Body & Wellness and Empowerment Life Coach of Strength Health & Empowerment Life Coaching Services.

I am also a Master Fitness Trainer and nutrition coach that provides key tools to help the community to not only lose weight, but fill them with the knowledge to maintain their health. Get rid of stigmas, answering questions, and providing key tools to balance life and health. Strength Health and Empowerment is secondary to my main brand UncoveringTheNewU.

I have developed a four-step process that reinforces the importance of goal setting to help understand the connection of physical and mental health and how it affects the development of self-esteem and building intrinsic motivation. In addition, I have experience in discussing all areas of being an athlete and building resilience, as I am also a Master Resiliency Trainer in the US Army, Sexual Assault Victim Advocate, and hold a Master's degree in Sports and Health Science with a minor in sport performance, pending my Doctorate in 2018 in Psychology.

Contact info:
Email: utnuinfo@gmail.com
Website: www.Uncoveringthenewu.com

Tell us about your business.

UncoveringtheNewU, LLC is a privately-owned fitness company that offers a variety of health and wellness services to all ages and genders. It is a company that believes health should be a main priority, and focuses on teaching and training individuals the proper way to maintain overall health and reach their goals through nutrition and effective physical exercise.

The sub-entity Strength, Health, and Empowerment Life Coaching Services offers an opportunity to anyone who is experiencing challenges in balancing their health and wellness. I have developed a four-step system to help them reach their goals of living life to its fullest potential.

As an entrepreneur and employee, what are some of the challenges you face with your business? Is being an employee slowing down your progress?

Not everyone is interested in fitness. Fitness is a marathon, not a sprint, and many seek quick results. As a natural built trainer, I do not do anything quickly. Permanent health results do not come overnight and many people aren't willing to invest in the commitment process. Business doesn't always go as planned because of this.

As an employee, I am always working. I am in the Army Reserves, work two jobs, and in school. Time is of the essence for me. I have to make do of every moment of my day. In the beginning, I used to take my business work with me to work. I would use my lunch period and breaks to draft ideas and programs. I was wearing myself out doing this. I found that just as I was setting aside time for my family and to work for other businesses, I needed to sit down and properly plan my business, as well. It took a long time to understand this key strategy.

Yes, being an employee does slow down my progress in my business. Since my business requires my presence, I can't do it from work. But, I am using my earnings to ensure I can take care of my priorities and provide for my family. Any money I receive from my business goes into savings.

When it comes to finances, what resources have you used to fund your business?

Currently, I am using my own finances to fund my business. I own all of my gym equipment and supplies. I am currently researching grants to help fund the marketing of my business.

Being an entrepreneur, how do you balance life and family when there seems to never be enough time in a day?

As crazy as it may seem, I actually write out all of my activities and assign them atime. I make my schedule every Sunday about what must get done each day, the order of their importance, and the hours they are to be completed. That is really the only way I can function, by holding myself accountable for every minute of my day. Now the golden question you may have is, *Do things always work this way?* Absolutely not. If for some reason time runs over or situations occur, I add that task to the next day. But, I complete the important items first. I learned to prioritize the needs of my business and the needs of my family, creating a happy medium.

What are some of the financial challenges you have faced in your personal life as you build your business? How did you overcome the challenges, and what strategies do you have in place to maintain a positive financial life?

I knew better than to use all of my money to invest without knowing if my business would generate more income. I do not currently face any personal financial issues. The only challenge I have now is gaining clientele to use the equipment and generate wealth. Since I have completed my gym, I've had to increase my marketing, develop new strategies, and invest more time in developing new programs.

What advice would you give someone who is an employee and entrepreneur but wants to seek entrepreneurship full-time ?

My advice is to ensure there is a proper plan in place. It is hard to gain success without a plan or program. In your plan, make sure you have paths to your success that include what you will need, how you will obtain what you will need, a budget, and sacrifices that will be made. Building a business comes with sacrifices. Sometimes they are huge, but worth it in the end.

Strategy #5:
How to Balance Time and Family with No Time Left in A Day

If you're like most people, even without building a business, there is not enough time in a day to live and run a life. No matter how many to-do lists you create, planners you fill up, and calendars you jot things down on, you still end the day with things undone. I used to manage my life by memory, making a mental note of everything I needed to do the next day or by the end of the week. This worked well for me for many years because it made me prioritize what was essential. I often told people, "If I forget, it's not important."

Rude!

Early on, I learned that everything in life is not a priority. Just because it's needed doesn't mean it needs to get done right away. However, as I grew older and wiser, I was forced to utilize my phone's calendar to maintain my children's schedules, my personal schedule, Pen Legacy's calendar, and my man's military schedule. Even though everything still requires some order of importance, I am learning that being organized and not having to rely solely on my brain's memory helps my overall mental health. In addition, having a visual of what is required makes it easier to balance out life and business, while maintaining a life for myself.

If you are like me, you are a mother, spouse or significant other, daughter, sister, niece, granddaughter, cousin, employee, sorority sister, Order of Eastern Star sister, church member, and friend. If you are a male reading this, just make every title masculine. If you noticed, I am a lot to a lot of people, and as you can see, I have not mentioned anything about myself. That's because a lot of times who we are and what we need is typically overshadowed by the many hats we wear.

I can remember being a new mother. Every time I saw someone, they immediately asked me, "How's Chris?" We would have a whole conversation about Chris, being a mother, about my job, and then the focus went on them. Never once did they ask, "Charron, how are you?" Did that ever happen to you? Sad to say, it still happens to me. However, now they ask, "What new books do you have out?" But never, "How are you doing?" Always talking about what you are and never shining light on *who* you are does something to your self-esteem and ability to keep pressing for yourself. If you're not careful, you will become immune to the "labels" while forgetting about yourself. This is why finding a balance in life is vital. In the last eight years, I have mastered five concepts that I find gives me the balance I need between work, family, fun, love, and Charron. They are:

- Accept That Everything Is Not a Priority
- Cut Your Losses
- Delegation Is Key
- Scheduling Saves Lives
- Know When to Shut Off Completely

Accept That Everything Is Not a Priority

My favorite mantra for myself is, *"You Can't Be Everything to Everybody. It Will Always Leave Nothing for Yourself."* I repeated this quote to myself for years, but it wasn't until I read the book *Essentialism* by Greg McKeown that I started living what I was saying. Before reading this book, I wouldn't make sure my calendar was clear before saying yes to something else. I was always "down for whatever". However, after taking Mr. McKeown's advice, I learned to be more selective when deciding what I saw asessential. I did not have to say yes to everything, and I did not have to be everywhere just because I was free. It's okay for me to regain control of my choices so I can channel my time, energy, and effort into making the highest possible contribution to the things that really matter.

> Greg states that, *"The Way of the Essentialist isn't about getting more done in less time. It's not about getting less done. It's about getting only the right things done. It's about challenging the core assumption of 'we can have it all' and 'I have to do everything' and replacing it with the pursuit of 'the right thing, in the right way, at the*

right time'. It's about regaining control of our own choices about where to spend our time and energies instead of giving others implicit permission to choose for us."

Understanding that everything is not a priority will free up time, save your mental and emotional health, and give you the opportunity to focus on what will benefit you. Removing "busy" work and replacing it with the "right" work is how I now operate my life and manage the many hats I wear. Plus, if you follow me on social media, you see I put myself first more. Taking ownership is how us #Bosses generate MASSIVE RESULTS. Not only do we own business(es), we own our lives and everything that transpires within it. Thus, finding what is essential is paramount because it holds the key to your balance and unwavering success.

Shift your mindset! The next time you're offered an opportunity or invitation, sit back and think, *How will this affect my overall bottom line?* The next time you feel the need to write content and get "stuff" done, I want you to ask yourself, *Is this the very most important thing I should be doing right now?* Or, *Will this work generate an immediate reward?* If the answer is no, then I want you to **C**arefully **A**ssess **R**eal **R**ealities (that bring) **E**ffective **R**esults.

Regardless if it's your job or your business, all of this will elevate and enhance your C.A.R.E.E.R, and if worked correctly, it will lead to a wealthy and life-fulfilled retirement. From this point on, everything you do has to be done for a purpose and foreseen results. Doing things today just to say you've done it is not always a great thing, because what you did last week is now considered obsolete, especially in this ever-changing society we live in. Plus, the spirit in which you completed the task can also affect the delivery of the product you are creating. So, I suggest you complete when needed and execute when necessary. Your energy will transfer better and your goals will be better met.

In addition, stop thinking YOU have to do it all! I'm here to dismantle that myth by saying, "No, you don't!" Even with all the advice I have given you so far in this book, only you can decide what is a priority. However, trying to build, brand, register, and execute all in one week is why you are exhausted and overwhelmed. Also, know what you need to delegate. Every task cannot and should not be done by you. Building a business takes time, and being able to comprehend that is how you enjoy the process and remain committed. Frustration begets Failure!

Cut Your Losses

How many of you are carrying baggage? Do you know that mental and emotional baggage drains you physically, causing you not to function at your fullest potential? Cutting your losses is another way to find time and balance in your life while building a business. When I got serious about making Pen Legacy an official business, I had to cut people, programs, "busy" work, friends, and excessive drama so I could get focused on the goal at hand. I didn't invest my time, energy, and finances in Pen Legacy and Charron Monaye just to say, "I did it!" My company and brand were created to generate results and build a legacy for myself and for the generations to follow. So, I needed to be in the right mindset to work effectively.

Also, being a writer, I knew I would lose readers if all I wrote was drama-filled stories with the same plot twists and storylines. As a reader, would you invest in a writer who wrote books that had the same message, with the only difference being the book covers? No! So, I needed new narratives and new experiences to make each book and stage play a new journey for you.

But how do you let go? For many, letting go in order to grow is hard because they are familiar and comfortable with the dysfunctions of their present life. Stepping into an unknown space can bring loneliness and create fear, but in that unknown space is where you will find everything you need to achieve everything you desire. Another reason why many people don't let go is because they want to bring everybody and everything with themas they elevate. To some point, I agree there is nothing wrong with pulling people up with you. I created an entrepreneur group that has enabled me to coach people and friends on how to meet me where I am in this business world. But, in doing this, I have learned that everybody doesn't want to do the work as much as they want the instant gratification (or should I say, fame). Others don't mind the work; however, they want your name all over it to give them the advantage. So, now, I find myself frustrated and upset with these people for their lack of honesty and truth, which causes me to be mentally drained when it comes time to do what I have to do for Pen Legacy.

You can't save everybody! You can't make everyone an entrepreneur. Better yet, entrepreneurship is not for everybody. As my mother always says, "Everybody is not meant to be rich." So, when bringing people with you, know their true intentions and control your personal interest or investment into their business. It's okay to show concern about them and their success, but you cannot care to the point where it ends up costing you to lose your sanity and keeps you from completing your deadlines.

In addition to cutting drama and people from your life, stop investing in things that you know won't lead you anywhere. (That last sentence would be a good one for you to highlight). This concept also aligns with the term "*sunk cost bias*" that I now use before saying yes to anything.

I've wasted countless amounts of money and time knowing that what I was doing was pointless, but I did it anyway because my schedule was clear and I had some "free money". Let me make this clear; a clean calendar means rest, and as an entrepreneur, no money is free. Every dime you have should be reinvested to level up your business. Your business should grow and that should be evident in your branding. So, spending with no clear return is a big no-no. People who do this are always in the red and working to generate more money to play catchup. Hell, I used to do it. Again, I am not offering any advice that I have not tried, which is why I am able to teach you what I am doing now with hopes that it will save you from spending thousands and taking seven years to get clear on your brand and business.

Delegation Is Key

We have already set the tone that you can't do everything yourself, and this is the point where you actually embrace and stand in the truth of it. As a start-up company, you may not be able to afford to hire a team, or you find yourself hesitating when it comes to trusting people to delegate work to. However, trying to do it all yourself is business suicide and can cause a nervous breakdown.

As I stated in previous chapters, I worked my business alone from 2009 to 2015, but being a writer, I did not need to delegate much except for editing and graphic design work. When I started my journey as a playwright, hiring a team was mandatory; it came with that industry. Running a play solo is virtually impossible. Even when it came to me publishing new authors, my editor and graphic designer were already in place, but then I needed to contract a printing company and book distributor. But, for some businesses, you will need to hire a full team to work behind the scenes to help you provide exceptional service. I know some speakers who require a whole entourage for their business. They have their personal assistant, booking agent, manager, make-up artist, stylist, content manager, attorneys, and accountant.

But how do you get all of this help when you are first starting out? You don't! You learn your business enough to know what things you can do and what needs to be delegated. When it comes to business setup, branding, business structure, and registering your business, I recommend you get professional help because, in my opinion, these four things need to be executed correctly. So, hiring a coach and a tax professional will teach you how to handle your tax matters correctly, how your business should operate, and how to create a business image that will attract clients.

Instead of hiring outsiders, some entrepreneurs utilize their family and friends to work with them, those who believed in their vision. For example, my oldest son has been my assistant since 2012. From book signings to traveling to events, he has always served and did not care if we made money or not. We have sat at book signings for hours and made no money, and other times, we went to book signings and sold out. Getting yourself a ride-or-die team mate is crucial. I have also summoned my mate to become my personal business counselor.

My man is a great supporter, listener, and partner when it comes to everything in the world of entrepreneurship. He has given me book topic ideas, quickly dismisses business ideas he feels aren't good, chin-checks me when I start to complain about working, and offers comfort when I share my frustrations about unpaid balances. That type of love and support for a business person is amazing, and even better, there is no price tag on his support. He is not an entrepreneur; however, he loves to read, so his advice as a reader helps propel me forward. Writing this book was his idea because he feels readers connect more to people who have lived the experience, are transparent, and use their testimony to educate others. He is very big on listening to people who have lived what they preach. He will be the one at a conference Googling the speaker's net worth to see if they are in a position to teach anybody how to become a millionaire. So, when I talked to him about the original idea for this book, which was being a successful entrepreneur, he told me, "No, *because you're still employed.*" He wasn't saying I'm not successful, but I am not a successful entrepreneur, alone. At first, I was in my feelings because he shot down my great idea, but then I thought, *Fine, I will add the word employed to the title*, and he approved. Now see, one of my coaches would have charged me for that piece of advice he gave me.

As you see, delegating does not always mean handing over work to others for them to do. It can be having a conversation, strategizing, and planning. I guarantee you the last thing my man wants to do after working twelve to fourteen hours a day is come home and be a business manager or coach. My rule of delating is, ***Pay for what you know you will destroy if you try to do it yourself***. That is how I determine what to delegate, e.g., hiring an accountant or graphic designer. When you understand the value of money and how it's needed for your business, you will become very selective on how you spend it. If you notice, a lot of billionaires don't look or live like their net worth. Not saying you can't have fun or live in luxury, but wasteful spending is bad for your budget. Don't bankrupt your business by thinking that's how you'll excel. Running a business on a budget is okay and very typical within the first couple of years, or until your business generates enough profits that will allow you to spend without ending up in the red. Delegate what you can and hire who you must. Just make sure it all serves a purpose in elevating your business.

Side note: While delegating, what should you do next? I, personally, learned every area of my business, from marketing to advertising, to content writing, to branding, to obtaining funding, to gaining traction in the marketplace, and to effective networking. I read books, signed up for free webinars, attended low-cost conferences, connected with people via Facebook and watched their live streams, and downloaded free e-books from their websites. Granted, all of this learning delayed me from executing, but being broke, it gave me time to learn. Most entrepreneurs will share this sentiment. In my opinion, a good time to learn is while starting out, even though you will be continuously learning as an entrepreneur. However, during this time, you are not totally consumed with trying to meet your customer's needs.

Scheduling Saves Lives

I know I said before that I used to keep a mental note of everything I had to do. However, I don't recommend that for anybody. I missed a lot of appointments and double booked myself alot. This made me look ineffective and unorganized. I even missed school programs for my children, but I don't think they minded much because they wouldn't always remind me. One way to balance time is by having a planner or some sort of calendar that keeps track of your events. I use my Google calendar for everything, and I even schedule time off on the 16th of each month where I dedicate to doing nothing. I call those my "Me-cations", which I will discuss in the next chapter. Planning and being realistic about your days and weeks will help you utilize your time better.

One of the things I do now that has helped me to be more productive is create "theme days". I have given each day a task. If I don't have any work that needs to get done that day, I use the time to do things pertaining to my personal life or just rest. For example, my calendar looks like this:

- ✓ **Social Media Sunday**
- ✓ **Content Monday**
- ✓ **Pitching Tuesday**
- ✓ **Publishing Wednesday**
- ✓ **Business Thursday**
- ✓ **Follow-Up Friday**
- ✓ **Sales Saturdays**

My hours of operation are 9a.m. to 3p.m. and 7p.m. to 9p.m., but only if I decide to hold a coaching session via Facebook Live at 7p.m. or 8p.m. Typically, I am working or writing throughout the day. This way, when I leave work, I am leaving all work for the day and coming home to be mommy, girlfriend, daughter, or just Charron. Now, I know everybody can't work on their business *while* at work, and that's okay. I couldn't always either, but when I couldn't, working from 9pm to 1- or 2am was my set schedule. If I had to write a book, my children understood that Mommy had to work right after work, and we would order dinner and discuss our day in seconds rather than minutes. Now that I have finished building my businesses, my calendar, even though still full, is manageable because I stretch out deadlines to allow myself "me time" and to plan my days according to the theme. I don't accept immediate projects if I can't give immediate results. I don't chase money and then stress on trying to complete it. Lastly, I only accept purposeful work that will excite me rather than something that feels like work.

Managing my days like this has helped me tremendously. Plus, it leaves me with time to do more with my kids, travel, and one of my favorite things to do, sleep. But, these rewards only come from strategizing your day, not accepting more than you can handle, and remembering that "busy" work won't get you repeat customers; it will only keep you marketing for new ones.

Know When to Shut Off Completely.

Even with everything I've learned, this lesson took me the longest to master, and at times, I am still guilty of not doing it. Knowing when to shut down is the hardest thing for any person nowadays. The way we look at life, there is always something that can be done, but for an entrepreneur, our way of thinking is heightened to, "There is always money that can be made." For me, anytime my laptop was off that meant I was losing money. If I was not posting, I was not selling and thus not making money. I would drive and text, walk and close deals. From the time I got up until the time I closed my eyes, I was working.

I had it bad!

Little did I know, I wasn't making money because all of that posting and talking. It only led me to being "busy". Sure, I would get work, but the opportunities never matured into anything bigger. It was like the one-and-done method, and even though that is wonderful in your personal life, it is bad for entrepreneurs. This concept meant I was not getting repeat customers. Half the time, I wasn't securing customers because I was working for free in exchange for exposure, and where did that exposure get me? Nowhere. Why? They never credited my name or my role in the work that I completed.

Starting over was inevitable and being broke became the new normal. Even when I did get money, I was still broke. I was so far in the negative that any money I received was used to pay the balances of the credit cards I had used to finance the work. That's another thing. Do not create massive credit card debt! Try not to max out credit cards when starting your business. You do not have to buy everything at once. Entrepreneurship is an investment and will cost you as long as you are in business. So, rushing to buy and pay for everything is damaging to your personal credit and may affect your ability to obtain business credit and loans later.

Okay, so back to the topic at hand. How do you shut down when you have productive work to do?

First, stick to your schedule. Don't work during times not allocated for your business. I know this may be hard for some of you, especially when you get a result-driven assignment and are eager to get started. But, are you providing your best in that moment? My brain is programmed to stop writing after 6 p.m. My editors can tell if I wrote during my allotted time because the content makes more sense and flows better. Pushing yourself can cause your work to be ineffective. Listening to your body and adhering to a schedule is vital to your success of delivering quality work, which in turn can guarantee repeat clients.

Secondly, believe the quote, *"If the opportunity is for you, it will be yours."* You don't always have to be accessible. If someone wants you on their team, they will leave you a message or text and wait for you to return their call. Now, don't be fooled to believe they will wait months to hear back from you, but they will give you a reasonable amount of time to respond. I believe anything I have to force is not meant to be. Me being available all day and night is not going to make everybody who follows me want to contact me. People visit, like, share, and comment on my pages everyday; some buy my products while others hire me to do work.

Now my virtual store and business website, www.penlegacy.com and www.CharronMonaye.com, are always open for business. The great thing about these websites is that the content and payment links generate sells and leads for me. This business set-up has allowed me to focus more on my personal life and maintain a love life. I am able to live, laugh, and love without fearing that my business is going to become irrelevant because I am not working it. Getting to the point where your business works for you without you having to sign online or be that annoying salesperson who hounds potential clients on your page is a blessing.

Lastly, your relationship and/or marriage requires it. I remember in a former relationship of mine hearing my mate complaining, "You are always working." At that time, it did not faze me because I was getting work and exposure. However, with me saying yes to everything, it created a lot of arguments in my relationship. He would argue with me because he wanted to spend time with me, and I would ignore him because I wanted my business to flourish. All I saw was Pen Legacy and Charron Monaye , but where did he fit in? I'm not going to say I regret my actions, because like many people who are eager to build and create something bigger than themselves, they shift their focus, but this is where being honest in the moment comes in. It was obvious that I did not have the time to nurture a relationship anymore. I found my peace in my writing. Even after he ended our relationship, I kept working and evolving Pen Legacy to add the publishing component to the brand and release new books.

However, it wasn't until I started the relationship I am in presently that I actually gave my past behaviors a second thought and realized he deserved my time minus the work, laptop, and cellphone. It's funny to me now, because when I am with him, my phone can ring and I will not answer it. When we're together, I don't get on Facebook or check email, and it doesn't bother me at all. Giving him my undivided attention is necessary, and for me, it's a much-needed break from work. Maturity and having the right man makes you change your whole mindset regarding life. I can have a deadline coming up, and I'll either push the date back or get the task done before I go see him just so I'm not working or thinking about it while there. When I board the plane, everything related to the work of Pen Legacy remains in Philadelphia. I guess it's one of the perks of having a long-distance relationship. I get to turn off being an entrepreneur and just be me when we are together. I must say, giving him what he needs and what I enjoy giving has kept our relationship strong and stress-free. Hopefully by the time you read this book, we'll be married and permanently living together. Feel free to email me for the update! (LOL!)

Doing any of these five concepts that I listed and mastered will help you balance out your time, afford you more time, and allow you time to enjoy life feeling less stressed and overwhelmed. After everything you have completed and learned thus far, I think it's time for a vacation. Now that you've learned how to balance your time and family, let's invite ourselves into the equation. Self-care is essential when working full-time and building a business. So, let's book a flight and I'll meet you there.

Strategy #6:
Self-Care Leads To Great Wealth

One of the disadvantages of being an entrepreneur is working 24/7,365 days a year. No days off. But, when you are an entrepreneur and still an employee, I recommend understanding the importance of self-care. In the last chapter, we discussed balancing work and family. In this chapter, we will look at your personal wellness. Working two full-time jobs can be mentally, emotionally, and physically taxing on your mind and body. Hence, life-altering health issues can manifest if you do not take the time to nurture yourself.

I know you're probably saying, "Charron, there's always something to do." I'm sure there is, but doing them while half tired and/or exhausted will not generate massive results. So, we need to change our mindset to incorporate a "Me-cation" once a month and a "Vacation" at least once a year. In addition, health and fitness, regular doctor visits, and getting plenty of sleep is just as important. Now, the "Me-cation" can be as simple as refraining from work and doing something you enjoy. This can be shopping, bowling, watching a movie, having dinner alone, or going to the park or beach solo. That alone time is needed to rebirth, rejuvenate, and realign with yourself. This allows the mind and body an opportunity to slow down (rest) and reconnect with your normal heart rate. This reconnecting and rest is necessary, because just like anything else, if you overwork it, it will breakdown and/or die. The only thing is, as humans, we can't get a new wire or battery when we breakdown. We either have to learn how to cope with being unable to move forward because of a delay or disability, or cease all operations because we can't perform at all. To prevent that, I will offer you some of advice on why vacations are important, how to stay physically energized, and how a "well-fed" mind can elevate your business, resulting in you getting closer to writing that resignation letter!

Vacation

If you're like me, you wear many hats, and if you're a mother or father, your hats are active duties that you can't keep up with at times. So how do you fit in a vacation? Before learning how important they are, I never took vacations. I had to work, probably didn't have time left to use at work, and most importantly, I could not afford it. You see, vacations cost money, and that was something I did not always have access to without using a credit card. So, vacations, as I knew them to be, were non-existing for me. Still, I found cost-effective ways to getaway for some much-needed peace and quiet, and a majority of the time sleep.

When you hear people say "The grind is real," or "The dream is free, but the hustle is sold separately,", know that the grind and hustle requires mentally strategizing your next move, even if you don't know what that is. It can be exhausting and frustrating to say the least! So,if you feel that way, just imagine what kind of tension and stress your body is experiencing. Therefore, mental rest days from work, "Me-cations", and vacations are mandatory.

What are some ways you can take a vacation on a budget, you ask? For me, I found a city where I could re-energize and have fun, and that was Manhattan, New York. Even with the rush and congestion, there is something about New York that gives me a sense of peace along with moments to just enjoy and relax. In addition, New York is only an hour-and-fifteen-minute drive from my house, so it only took some gas and tolls to get there. Manhattan became my go-to place for a vacation, even if only for a weekend. It was my time away to just be quiet. Or, I would drive down to Atlantic City or Wildwood, New Jersey because it's something about looking out into the horizon over the ocean. That scenery offered so much motivation and comfort. Imagine sitting on the beach and looking out at the water, birds flying carelessly and the sun is shining bright. That's a peace like no other.

Places like that are my run-to spots, and in them, I've experienced moments of rejuvenation. In addition, I've become addicted to getting massages. The relaxation I receive from them on top of the peace I get from taking vacations/"Me-cations" have me with a fresh pair of eyes and a new heart pattern when I return home. Also, I love driving on the highway, not during rush hour, though. We are elevating peace, not pain. I love the restaurant Waffle House, but there isn't a Waffle House in the area where I live. We patronize IHOP, and I'm over their food seriously. The closest Waffle House to me is straight down I-95 on the border of Delaware and Maryland, which is forty-five minutes away from me. But, you guessed it. I will drive to Waffle House, eat, and drive back home, paying tolls and everything. To others, it's wasting money, but to me, that drive gives me time to just think. Plus, I get to put on a mini concert in the car while looking forward to indulging in some awesome waffles and eggs. It's the little moments for myself like this that add up to big wins in my business.

So, you see, you don't have to spend thousands of dollars to go to some island or travel around the world to find downtime. You do have to know your sacred places, though. However, if you're the kind of person who has to travel to find peace, then I suggest you have your money in order, because there's nothing worse than going on vacation to get rejuvenated, only to come back home to bills and stress. It's almost like the vacation was needed, but you can't spare the expense of taking one. If I'm going to spend money to go away, that moment better stay with me until my next vacation. To me, temporary highs are good, but a high with longevity keeps me producing and elevating.

Health & Fitness

I know many people don't enjoy talking about health and fitness because it involves cutting out the things you love to eat that are bad for you and leaving the gym sore after working out, but it's mandatory. A personal trainer used to tell me, "You are what you eat," and me not caring, I would shoot back with, "Well, it's better to be soul food than hungry." But, with everything these companies are putting in and doing to our food, from pasteurizing to spraying pesticide chemicals and cloning, do we really know what we're eating anymore? Even though I am not a vegan, I follow a protein diet and drink more water than sugary drinks. Don't get me wrong, I still eat my soul food, but everything now is in moderation. Just because I see it doesn't mean I have to eat it, and trust me, it takes discipline and self-constraint. However, with changing my diet, I feel less bloated and weighed down, which is always amazing because I am always on the run. My handy, dandy vanilla protein shake keeps me going just like my former addiction to Pepsi. Plus, when I go to the doctor's, my vitals, cholesterol, blood pressure, sugar levels, and every other number they look for is normal. Being in my forties, this is very important to me.

Health is wealth!

You can only produce what you can work to achieve, and if you're living an unhealthy lifestyle, there will be problems forthcoming.

In addition to eating right, embrace the idea of fitness. Now, I am not promoting getting ripped as if you're about to enter a body-building competition, but being in shape is key to maintaining a business, a household, your health, and everything else on your plate. How many of you run up a flight of steps and are out of breath when you reach the top? If you raised your hand, you know it's time to change that, right? If you can't run up some steps, how can you run a business? Sad to say, there will be some running involved, whether it's running to a meeting or running to speak at an event because traffic backup made you late. What would people think if you ran into a conference so winded that they had to move your spot to speak so you could have time to catch your breath? Real bosses run cute, then get on the stage and produce. My personal trainer gives me a monthly workout to do in order to get my body prepared and my mind right.

Secret #1: When you work out to music, it enhances the moment because you forget about the pain and focus on the purpose. Create a workout playlist and watch your attitude towards fitness change. My workout playlist is "Fade" by Kanye West, only because I channel my inner Teyana Taylor, "Dreams and Nightmares" by Meek Mills, anything by Jay-Z or DMX, and "Who Runs the World" by Beyoncé. I even work out at home. I don't need a gym to keep my body in shape. I just need my music and a clear vision.

I want to share eight fitness tips from my personal trainer, Kenneth Nelson Jr. He's the owner of FitZonFit, an exercise physiologist, and a certified Master Fitness Trainer who helps me maintain my desire to workout. He taught me the importance of it and keeps me on the right track when it comes to what to eat and how much.

✓ Fitness Tip #1: Form is everything! If your form is off, you are bound for injuries.

✓ Fitness Tip #2: Portion control is the key to weight loss. Serving sizes shouldn't be larger than the palm of your hand.

✓ Fitness Tip #3: Muscle burns fat! Strength train! You don't have to lift heavy; you just have to lift consistently.

✓ Fitness Tip #4: Fitness has four components: Strength, Endurance, Balance, and Flexibility.

✓ Fitness Tip #5: Speed is only accomplished through proper technique. The better the technique, the faster you will become.

✓ Fitness Tip #6: Cardio regulates the density of your body fat, but you need strength training to keep the density down.

✓ Fitness Tip #7: The body requires three nutrients: Carbohydrates, Fats, and Proteins. The body needs carbs for energy, fats for warmth, and proteins to aid with recovery and repair. Here are some examples for each:

- Carbs (Complex)– Breads, Pastas, and Starches
- Carbs (Simple)– Fruits and Veggies
- Fats – Nuts and Dairy
- Proteins – Meats and Beans

✓ Fitness Tip #8: In order to reach your fitness goals, you need to embrace the process. There is NO PROGRESS without PROCESS.

Health is wealth and fitness is key. By applying this way of thinking to your lifestyle, you'll add value to your growth and keep yourself in alignment to generate massive results when it's "game time."

Plenty of Sleep

Have you ever heard someone say "I'll sleep when I die"? People say this to justify why they stay up 24 to 72 hours straight to get the job done. Now, I don't always get 8 to 10 hours of sleep, but even when I was building my business, I didn't stay woke 48 or 72 hours. There were times when I did stay up 24 hours because I had a deadline to meet, but that wasn't because I wanted to grind it out. It's because I didn't manage my time effectively. When I was working in the music industry, producers used to always tell me, *"Hits are made at night."* But, with working a full-time job, being a mom, and trying to write, the only hits being made at night was my head against the pillow. So, I had to create a plan that allowed me to manage my time better, while getting more than three hours of sleep at night.

Before we move forward, let's discuss why sleep is so important. According to the U.S. Department of Health and Human Services, "Sleep plays a vital role in good health and well-being throughout your life. Getting enough quality sleep at the right times can help protect your mental health, physical health, quality of life, and safety. During sleep, your body is working to support healthy brain function and maintain your physical health." Think about it this way:

✓ Sleep helps your brain work properly. While you're sleeping, your brain is preparing for the next day. It's forming new pathways to help you learn and retain information.
✓ Sleep plays an important role in your physical health. For example, sleep is involved in healing and repairing your heart and blood vessels. Ongoing sleep deficiency is linked to an increased risk of heart disease, kidney disease, high blood pressure, diabetes, and stroke.
✓ Getting enough quality sleep at the right times helps you function well throughout the day. People who are sleep deficient are less productive at work and school. They take longer to finish tasks, have a slower reaction time, and make more mistakes.

Now that you understand how lack of sleep affects your physical and mental health, how do you think it will affect your business? How can you be successful at being a boss when you're always TIRED? This goes back to you being the brand. When you step out the house, people are not looking at you as a human being; they are judging you as a business owner, author, singer, etc. They are looking at your appearance. Are you leaning over or standing up straight? Are your eyes half-shut or open wide? Are you smiling? Do you have dark circles or bags under your eyes? They are examining you from head to toe.

In case you didn't know, sleep plays a part in how you show up in the world, and since we're all trying to write resignation letters, you must be on point when it comes to showing up. Your strut must be fierce, confidence on fleek, and mindset on fiyah in order for people to believe that you quitting means you got this and your business is #winning. The key to getting proper sleep is managing your time and creating a lifestyle that promotes sleep. In the December 16, 2016, edition of *Entrepreneur Magazine*, Rose Leader wrote an article titled, "Entrepreneur's Best Advice for Good Sleep". In this article, she gives entrepreneurs fifteen tips from Entrepreneur.com writers and contributors to help you start getting enough sleep every night. For the sake of reading, I will offer you the eight that I have incorporated into my life and that I share with my coaching clients.

Trim down your workplace duties. Whether you're launching a new business or starting a position at a new company, it's vital to set aside time to sleep. Evaluate your workload, prioritize the most important things, and figure out what you can hold off on or pass along to co-workers who have more time. Prioritizing sleep starts with prioritizing your workday.

Stop drinking caffeine after lunch. It's okay to indulge in a cup of joe in the morning, but it's important to refrain from consuming any caffeinated drinks in the afternoon or evening. If you do, you're not only at risk of having trouble falling asleep but staying asleep, as well.

Relax before bed. Take at least ten minutes before bed to relax. This could be through meditation or yoga. Doing something that focuses on your breathing will calm your mind and reduce stress to ensure a good night's sleep.

Turn off your phone. To avoid distractions at night, whether that means incoming calls or the temptation to go on Facebook, turn off your phone before catching some zzz's.

Your bed is for sleeping only. Don't bring work to bed with you or do any other activities in bed, such as watching Netflix or scrolling on Facebook. As a matter of fact, stay out of your bedroom unless you're going to sleep.

Listen to your body. No matter how many articles tell you to wake up early in the morning, the truth is not everyone is a morning person. Everyone is different when it comes to sleep. That's why it's vital to listen to your body's needs. If you force yourself to wake up early, you may not be able to get your best work done because your mind is not fully awake yet. Pay attention to when your body is tired and figure out the best time for you to get a good night's sleep.

Rethink your diet. Cutting out sugars and highly processed foods will help you get a sound night's sleep. These foods do harm to your metabolism and insulin levels, which directly impact your sleep. Also, refrain from eating a big meal two hours before going to bed.

Create a healthy sleep schedule. Committing to a sleep schedule is vital to ensure you get a certain number of hours of sleep each night of the week. To get started, set an alarm at night to remind you to start getting ready for bed and another alarmto wake you in the morning.

Regular Healthcare Visits

As an entrepreneur, you would be surprised how much extra stress you add to your day.

➢ Being an entrepreneur, you have the responsibility of dealing with clients, collecting payment for unpaid invoices, marketing and promoting your business, and let's not mention having to smile even when tired. Your body is worn out.

➢ As an employee, you commute to and from work, put in 8 to 12 hours a day at a job, and try to maintain your sanity. Your mind is exhausted.

➢ As a regular person, you have to take care of home and your family, which includes everything from paying bills, to cooking dinner, to helping the children with their homework and putting them to bed. Your body and mind are drained. It seems never-ending.

Are you exhausted after reading all of that? Now imagine the kind of damage you are doing to your body. The stress, the strain, the lack of, and mental breakdown will eventually make you want to tap out. Keeping up with your health by visiting your physician is golden. Many entrepreneurs struggle with this because the cost of insurance is expensive, and even though having it is required, affording it is a challenge. So, many entrepreneurs go without and suffer as a result, but is this healthy?

Nine times out of ten, when you experience pain, it is your body's way of trying to tell you something is wrong, and there's only so much Ibuprofen will do if the problem is bigger than you think. Since I have yet to find myself a rich husband to put me on their health insurance plan, it's the reason I still maintain employment. For me, the cost of paying for health care compared to the amount of "profit" I make would leave me in a deficit. You see, I manage my business based on profit potential not revenue, whereas some people live for revenue. Revenue is good, but I am way more interested in what I have left after expenses are paid. That's the difference between revenue and profit:

- ✓ **Revenue** is the amount of money that a company receives during a specific period, including discounts and deductions for returned merchandise. It is the top line or gross income figure from which costs are subtracted to determine net income.

- ✓ **Profit** is a financial benefit that is realized when the amount of revenue gained from a business activity exceeds the expenses, costs, and taxes needed to sustain the activity.

As you read earlier, I operated my business in the red for years, so adding the extra expense of insurance would have made me throw in the towel a long time ago. Presently, I am price to profit, which has given me the advantage to see more of a profit. Thus, I can add more expenses, if necessary. However, for many entrepreneurs, they are not operating with a profit or capital, so as a result, they are forced to go without. If you're a mother, a sacrifice you can't bear is your children's healthcare for your business; it's not even up for discussion. But, regardless of who you are, entrepreneur or employee, regular visits to your physician, dentist, and optometrist should be just as important to you as walking into your bank.

You can't be any good to anyone if you're always sick. Whether you're an entrepreneur, an employee, or both, make the appointments and go. If you're an entrepreneur, here's some good news: the government allows you to deduct 100 percent of the amount you pay for both medical and dental insurance if you report a net profit on Schedule C, C-EZ, or F. But, please make sure you can pay for the insurance without bankrupting yourself.

Are You Living and Operating Your Best Self?

This chapter is full of self-care information; however, the coach in me will not let you walk away without a 30-day timeout schedule. I have to make sure YOU are in alignment and prepared for the mountains and valleys of this journey. So, this section will be for your upgrade and to make sure everything in your life is in order. This is extremely important because, again, if you are not together, your business will not be either. You are a reflection of what you represent.

I tell everyone who publishes under my publishing company that nobody buys your book or really cares what you have to offer. They do, however, care and respect your story, your movement, and your authenticity. So, if you have a business helping people with their finances, your credit score better be 800 or higher. If you are a real estate agent but still renting, there is seriously a problem. You are your brand! You represent your business! So, use the next 30 days and pulse check your life. We cannot call ourselves entrepreneurs, or even more leave our jobs, if our home, inner being, and lives are not prepared. Now, I must warn you that some days will be relaxing and other days will be frustrating, but know if you do the work, come Day 31, you will know exactly what you need to keep working on in order to meet your goal.

Day 1

Physical Makeover. It's time to go through your wardrobe and carefully pay attention to your appearance. Your appearance plays a big part in how you feel about yourself on a day-to-day basis, or how you view yourself from the inside and out. So, today, go get your hair done, get those manicures and pedicures, and go shopping for clothes and accessories with a splash of color to brighten your wardrobe. I want you to look in the mirror and notice something different about yourself. The person you saw when you woke up this morning should not be the same person you smile at when it's time to go to sleep this evening.

Day 2

Rebirth yourself with love, confidence, enjoyment, happy thoughts, and positive images. Speak life back into yourself. Manifest the thoughts you know will keep your attitude positive. Let no one get under your skin. Control your feelings and think only of things that will enhance your day. You become what you think. So, today, it's all about engraving a new mentality! Think it! Say it! Live it!

Day 3

Step outside of your "box"! We all have this area in our lives where we only do what's comfortable, but living starts when you are most uncomfortable. When you're familiar, you exist, but when you're unfamiliar, you explore, learn, and go above and beyond to reach your destination. Today, do something outside of the norm. It can be doing something you've never done, trying something you've never tried, or wearing something you've never worn. It may seem strange at first, but after enjoying the experiences, I assure you it will be worth it.

Day 4

It's okay to be selfish with your life. Stop giving people an all-access pass to your life. Stop telling social media, your co-workers, and anyone who will listen the details of your personal business. It's one thing to share your testimony to inspire someone else; it's another thing to be gossiping and boasting for the sake of hearing yourself talk. Everything ain't for everybody, and unless they are willing to invest (and assist), they should have no say. Move in silence; it's harder for people to throw up roadblocks if they don't know what you are doing and when you are doing it.

Day 5

Fitness is maintaining a healthy life. Physical activity and proper nutrition are two of the most important elementsto a healthier lifestyle. Regular exercise will maintain the performance of your lungs and heart, efficiently burn off excess calories, and keep your weight under control. Another benefit of physical activity is that it decreases the risk of heart disease, stroke, colon cancer, diabetes, and high blood pressure. Good nutrition is just as important because it can also help you reach and maintain a healthy weight, reduce your risk of chronic diseases, and promote your overall health. So, today, I would like you to plan and execute the following: 1) obtain a gym membership; 2) join a Zumba class; and 3) meet with a nutritionist or research healthier food choices. With regular exercise and nutritious foods, your energy, stamina, and health will improve.

Day 6

Health is Wealth! Today, your task is to make appointments to see your primary care physician, optometrist, and dentist. Healthcare is important, and maintaining your health requires timely follow-ups with the doctors noted above. This will help with early detection of many viruses, diseases, or life-threatening agents. In order to be productive in business, your body must be operating at its best. Make your appointments today so you can live a long, long, long life.

Day 7

Forgiveness is not for them, but for you. You will never fully be able to move on with living your life if you continue to harbor ill will against those who hurt you, abandoned you, denied you, or have forsaken you. So, today, I want you to face the pain you're holding on to by either calling that person, writing a letter to them, or speaking it out loud in a silent room. Tell them how they hurt you, how it made you feel, and then say, "But, I forgive you." In addition, I want you to forgive yourself for the damage you may have caused yourself by holding onto those resentments for so long.

Day 8

Do something that will excite you. If you are an employee, mother, wife, father, husband, member of an organization, etc., you know there is never enough time in a day for YOU. After you tend to everyone else's needs, there is no time remaining for you...at least no awake time. Today, I want you to cancel, reschedule, or otherwise adjust your schedule so that YOU can do something for YOU. It can be as simple as sleeping in, going for a walk, having a solo lunch, or getting your hair done. No matter what you choose, it must be all about you.

Day 9

Elevate your life! When you were a young girl or boy, you had a dream of becoming something, living in a particular house, driving a particular car, and having a certain amount of money. Think about what your younger self wanted and what your older self has or does not have. Did you make your younger person happy? Did you accomplish that dream? If not, today, I want you to figure out why or why not, and make a plan to work towards achieving at least two of your childhood desires.

Day 10

Reading is Fundamental! Many people say reading is relaxing as well as healing to some. It allows your mind to wander, gain insight on different topics, and enjoy a great adventure without ever leaving the house. Sometimes a book can take you out of your reality and place you within a story, giving you the excitement and fulfillment of experiencing something greater than your immediate surroundings. In addition to mental stimulation, reading increases your grasp of knowledge, and knowledge is definitely power! It gets no better than that! Take time to read today.

Day 11

Re-evaluate your circle of friends. Being linked with like-minded people is important to your growth as a person. I know you've heard people say, "You are the company you keep." Well, today, look at the people who you associate with and make sure they are beneficial to you in some way. If they are not adding value to your life, they are hindering your progress. Surround yourself with people who support your vision, are willing to travel with you during the course, and understand the importance of you reaching your destination. Being successful will require that the people closest to you at least support your journey, even if they do not understand or agree with the direction you have chosen for yourself.

Day 12

Build your creditworthiness. As I'm sure you know, we live in a credit-driven society. Most things of importance that we need, such asa car, house, apartment rental, student loan, utilities, cell phone, and much more, requires us to have credit, and good to excellent credit at that! If you want low interest rates, you need to have a relatively high credit score. Today, I want you to take a step towards building your credit and join myfico.com. This will allow you to monitor your credit reports and scores. Additionally, I suggest you request a copy of your credit report (if you haven't done so within the last year) from all three companies and check them for accuracy. Your credit is your report card that companies review when you look to borrow money, apply for credit, and secureservices. If your credit is not where it should be, you definitely should start taking steps to fix it. Here are some websites to get you started:

- **www.creditkarma.com** ~ Instantly receive your free credit score and free credit reports online.
- **www.annualcreditreport.com** ~ Get a free copy of your credit report every 12 months from each credit reporting agency.

Day 13

Invest NOW in your retirement. I don't know about you, but I want to retire long before I turn sixty-five so I can enjoy life. I also know if I don't plan for it, I will probably be working until the day the good Lord calls me home. We can start planning for the future while we have the time and opportunity. I encourage you to research TODAY the investment and retirement opportunities that are available to you, either through your employer or privately funded entities. If you don't already have a 401K or 403B program set up, contact your Human Resources representative and ask about starting one. Meet with a financial planner and see if he/she can come up with a forecast for your future. Then identify ways to prepare for it and the goals you need to set to achieve that preparation. When you plan and prepare early, you can rest and enjoy later.

Day 14

Family love is the best love! I used to say family are our first friends in life. They gossip; they support us; they can be naysayers, and they are the first group of people with whom we learn day-to-day interaction. Since we can't pick them, we still have to love them, either in close quarters (for those who we get along with) or from a distance (for those who we have less affinity). Today's task is to call, Skype, visit, or have dinner with one of your family members. Take the time to laugh, cry, catch up, or to simply say I love you. No matter how crazy or messy they are, family are the ones who know you the best, and the ones who will be missed and who will miss you when all is said and done.

Day 15

Apologize to yourself for hurting yourself! Removing baggage is vital to your growth and your ability to maintain your progress. As you continue to work on forgiving those who have hurt you, you must also forgive yourself for the self-inflicted pain you suffered. People only do to us what we allow, and as much as we want to blame others for our emotional state, we have to look at the role we ourselves played in the hurt that we suffered. So, today, write a letter to your old self acknowledging and apologizing for everything you put YOU through. After you write the letter, read it aloud while standing in front of a mirror and looking at yourself. Once you finish reading it, look at yourself and say, "I'm SORRY."

Day 16

Improve your prayer life! If you're a spiritual person, you have heard the saying, "Prayer changes things." Prayer gives you hope, faith, and strength to press forward in life. When was the last time you considered your prayer life and how it affects your peace of mind? When was the last time you said a prayer? When was the last time you approached your higher power in prayer for guidance, direction, or just to say thank you? Spiritual growth is just as important as physical health. There is power in prayer for those who believe, and there is peace in knowing that your needs will be met by that higher power who hears you. So, today, pray for everything, give thanks, and maintain your connection with your higher power.

Day 17

Speak life into your existence. I know we covered this area before, but we can never have too much of a good thing, right? And positive affirmations are always helpful. Speak to your success. Speak to your love. Speak to your breakthrough. Speak to your transformation. Speak to your healing. Speak to your peace. Speak to your increase. Speak to your clarity. Speak to your confidence. Use your words to infuse your soul. Infuse your body, mind, and spirit with positive energy through positive words. Your thoughts become your words; your words become your action; and your actions become your reality. So, start positively so you can arrive at positivity.

Day 18

Take a vacation. Like many of us, you probably need a break from day-to-day life issues and a vacation from the everyday hustle and bustle. I don't know your financial status, but I do know everyone can make a way to take a needed break to regroup and readjust. If you can't plan a 5-star vacation on the beach, plan a staycation, take a day trip, or work for a half day and then go home and sleep for a few extra hours. I do it every chance I get. I have no problem going to New York, staying overnight in a hotel,and then coming back home the next day. It may sound crazy, but when I return, I am so rejuvenated. Try it…you'll thank me later. Commit to making time to execute at least one type of break within the next month.

Day 19

Build multiple streams of revenue. Trying to live comfortably requires more money than we usually have in our accounts. Having multiple streams of revenue helps to ensure that you have cash on hand, and it is helpful in enabling you to build a savings account. If you possess a gift, talent, or skill, allow it to work for you. If you like to write, pen a book and sell it. If you like cars, learn how to repair them. If you like to coach people, become a life coach and charge for your services. Instead of throwing away your old clothes, start an online clothing business through pre-created websites. There are multiple ways you can receive revenue, but you have to find your passion and make it work. As you help others, you are actually earning income to help yourself. Win-win, right? Pick an idea, then work to see if you can build that idea into one that will bring you income.

Day 20

Attend professional networking events or join professional organizations. Growth in our professional lives can have a huge impact on our overall life because it gives us 1) a greater feeling of accomplishment, 2) job stability, and 3) a higher level of productivity, which can lead to advancement opportunities. When your professional life is in order, your overall sense of success is heightened. Today, search for and plan to attend some professional networking events. Research what it will take to join one or two professional organizations (preferably those related to your current field or business interests) so you can connect and network with others with the same interests and who have access to resources that you might not have knowledge of.

Day 21

Tear down those walls. Having walls, boundaries, limitations, and restrictions on your life will only hinder you from growing into the person you are destined to be. Examine the limits and restrictions you are placing on yourself. Make sure you are not permitting others in your life to place limitations on you unknowingly. Wherever there is doubt, erase it! Wherever there is fear, remove it! Wherever there are lines drawn in the sand, walk over them! Identify two things that might be holding you back or limiting your access. Plan to eliminate those things, and set a timeline to address and execute the plan. Move forward with that plan within the timeframe you have established.

Day 22

Plan a romantic evening. Showing love is extremely important in both a relationship and for yourself. When interacting within the life of another, you must take time out to love on, love with, and do loving things to remind your partner that they are appreciated, cared for, and needed. For those who are single, take time out to show the same appreciation for yourself! Treat yourself to something special, buy yourself flowers, or get a massage. Romancing yourself is just as necessary as it is for two people who are maintaining the romance between them. Take the time to plan something for this week that will show appreciation, whether for your significant other or for yourself.

Day 23

Estate planning. Ensure your affairs are in order BEFORE the time it is needed. Focus on life insurance, wills, living wills, trust funds, and power of attorney. What will happen should you pass? If you leave this earth today or tomorrow, will your family have the money to pay for your funeral? Will they be able to distribute your assets without fighting? As we focus on living, we must also prepare for death. Losing you is going to be a traumatic moment, but having to raise money, fight with other loved ones, and debate over property can add trauma to an already stressful event. Prepare your family for the inevitable and give them the gift of your preparation. Today, take the time to research obtaining life insurance if you don't already have it or review your life insurance policy if you do. Update your will or create one. Ensure that your family will know what your wishes are in the event that you are no longer able to verbalize them. Contact an estate planning attorney and start planning.

Day 24

Pray for Increase in your Life! Daily, we are reminded that we can never settle for less when we are deserving of and desire so much more. As my mother would say, "A closed mouth don't get fed." So, today, we are going to pray for an increase in our environment, finances, energy, understanding, patience, vision, and love. The Bible says "Ask and it shall be given unto you; seek and ye shall find." As you pray for increase, pray also for the wisdom to put that increase to good use and for the ability to be a good steward with the increase that comes. Praying is encouraged.

Day 25

Step out on Faith! Today, I want you to consider things you want to do but have always been afraid to do. Think on these things and prepare yourself to meet a challenge. Choose ONE THING right now that you will strive to accomplish. And TRY! So what if you fail! So what if you finish last! Your main focus is simply to try. It doesn't matter whether or not you actually finish; what matters is that you TRY. Right NOW, identify something, see it through, and be proud of your effort. You can do it!

Day 26

Volunteer your time. Life can sometimes have us so busy that we forget the importance of volunteering our time to help those in need, inspiring others, or making a difference in the lives of others through community service. "It takes a village to raise a child," is the statement that for so long has held our communities together. That statement still holds true today. With the unstable economy, homelessness, identity crises, and mental health issues running rampant throughout our communities, volunteering time to help those in need is one of the most rewarding things you can do. There are many organizations that can use your skills. I challenge you to pick one, then take the time to give back to someone less fortunate.

Day 27

Find ways to CUT your expenses! Some people live paycheck to paycheck, making just enough to survive, while others are barely surviving. Today, we are going to find ways to cut our expenses. You cannot live only to pay bills, and being broke is not beneficial. So, it's time to find ways to save money. Look at all of your personal expenses and see if you can downsize or cancel anything. Identify what items are needs and what are non-essentials. Write out all expenses, down to the smallest item. Pick one item that can be eliminated and remove that expense today. The funds that were used to pay for that item should be redirected into a savings account. It might seem like a stretch for a bit, but it's doable and will feel so good in the long run when you see your savings grow.

Day 28

Learn about and consider investing in stock. Investing in stock may seem risky to some people, but to others, it has been a source of great financial gain. Investing is not a "rich man's game" as people often assume it to be. For those who are interested in learning about investing, there are many opportunities to start small and cautiously. There are also opportunities for those who desire to be more aggressive in their investing. Today, I challenge you to take a moment to gain some knowledge regarding the tool of investing and how it can be used to work for you. Research what your first steps would be if you were to begin to establish an investment portfolio. You don't have to actually invest if you decide that it is not for you, but at least you will have the information to come back to should you change your mind.

Day 29

Write a personal mission statement. Think of your journey as a business, as a brand. If you had to sell yourself to someone, what would your two-minute pitch consist of? Today, write your mission statement. Think about: 1) Why you exist and your reason for being, 2) What you have to offer and to whom or what you are devoted to, and 3) How you are committed to maintaining your legacy. After you have given these questions some thought and sketched some things out, write your statement and post it where you will always see it! Having a visual of your mission, purpose, and vision will better help you remain focused.

Day 30

Practice Self-Compassion. Today is all about loving yourself through your words and removing every negative phrase, word, or comment ever directed towards you from your mentality. Feeding yourself negativity is never healthy, and it's just as damaging as if you were physically harming yourself. Instead of criticizing, belittling, or telling yourself how unworthy you are, provide strength, speak life, and be kind to your mental and emotional being. Once you view yourself as being marred, you damage your self-esteem and self-confidence. So, today, I encourage you to heal the way you view yourself. Be compassionate towards yourself and lift your self-esteem with positive talk. Write out a list of hurtful words and negative feelings you have harbored over the years. After completing that task, I want you to tear up the paper into the smallest pieces possible and throw it in the trash. As you remove those negative thoughts, allow your personal mind space to refill with positivity.

You Made It!!!

"I Want to Quit My Job"
Entrepreneurial Conversation...

Khristina Barnes, MSAC offers more than fifteen years of experience in auditing, accounting, and individual and small business taxation.

Mrs. Barnes is currently the Budget Analyst Supervisor for the City of Philadelphia and its related entities, as well as a consultant specializing in taxation accounting services. Her responsibilities include overseeing all financial and grant accounting transactions, as well as preparing and monitoring program budgets that total approximately $5.3 million. Prior to this opportunity, Khristina worked in various positions within the government and public utility sector. In 2010, she founded and created KMB Tax Services, LLC, where she serves her community by offering tax preparation for individual and small business, bookkeeping for small businesses, tax planning and consultation, payroll services, and financial educational seminars.

Khristina Barnes graduated from West Chester University where she obtained a Bachelor's Degree in Accounting; she also earned her Master's in Accounting with a concentration in Taxation from Strayer University. She is a member of the National Association of Tax Preparers.

Contact info:
Phone: 267-973-6539
Email: khristinabarnes@kmbtaxservices.com
Website: kmbtaxservices.com

Tell us about yourself and your business.

I work for the Department of Public Health for the City of Philadelphia. I am a Budget Analyst Supervisor for the Maternal Child Family Health Division. I oversee financial and grant transactions, and prepare and monitor program awards totaling $5.3 million. In addition to working for the City of Philadelphia, I own a full-service tax preparation and accounting company called KMB Tax and Accounting Services, LLC. Our company provides tax preparation, accounting, consultation, financial coaching, and bookkeeping services for individuals and small businesses. Ever since I started KMB Tax and Accounting Services, I have been on a quest to educate college students, new mothers, and entrepreneurs about the importance of saving, tax investing, and debt management. In addition, I enjoy educating minority small business owners on tax deductions and cost-effective ways to operate and manage a profitable business.

As an entrepreneur and employee, what are some of the challenges you face with your business? Is being an employee slowing down your progress?

Some of the challenges I face as an entrepreneur is money, marketing, and time. As an entrepreneur, you need to have money. Money to learn all the aspects of having a business, as well as having money to operate my business. I prioritize all expenses. It's rough, but I do it. I also try to make sure that with any expenses I pay for, I sell a service to pay for it. I really struggle with social media. Everything I learned thus far about gaining exposure says you have to market your business on social media. I must admit, I have gotten four new clients since I've been posting on Facebook and Twitter. I just have to set aside more time to focus on my marketing campaigns and possibly hire someone to handle it for the business.

I think being employed is slowing me down a little. I mean, I'm at work for approximately eight hours a day. If I did not have a full-time job, I would utilize all those hours during the day for my business. Since I do have a full-time job, I work on my business during the evening. I may sneak in some hours during the day after I finish my assigned task at work. But, mostly, I work on KMB Tax and Accounting Services on the weekends and during the evening.

Having a successful business, why haven't you quit your job yet?

I haven't quit my job because I have not earned my current salary from KMB yet. This year, I can honestly say I see myself quitting my job sooner than I originally planned. I originally gave myself roughly five to eight years. I have student loans that I would like to pay off before quitting my job.

Being an entrepreneur, how do you balance life and family when there seems to never be enough time in a day?

It always seems like there isn't enough time in a day, but there is. I try and plan a lot. Being married with two kids, having to take them to their activities, and having a business requires a lot of planning and scheduling. I even plan our meals, family outings, and date nights, along with meeting with clients. It's a lot, but I found a system that works, and you will, too. The only thing I am not consistent with is scheduling personal time, but I'm working on it.

During your journey as an entrepreneur, what have you had to sacrifice so you can build your business?

I would say money and sleep. I used to have a set bedtime. Since I have expanded my business to include additional services, I've been staying up late to attend to the business. For example, the other day, I was determined to be in the bed by 10:00p.m. I did my nightly routine (laid clothes out for the kids and myself, and took out meat to defrost for tomorrow's dinner), then I looked over at my laptop and said, "You need to finish your book and update your website." Needless to say, I did not go to bed until 1:00a.m. I was tired the next day, but I felt accomplished. The feeling was amazing. Once I made the finishing touches on the book, I was so excited. Not only did I stay up late, but I found myself having a hard time winding down so I could fall asleep after all of that. So, you will make a lot of sacrifices while building your business. Just know it is well worth it.

What advice would you give someone who is an employee and entrepreneur, but wants to seek entrepreneurship full-time?

I would tell them to keep pressing onto their goal and to never give up! Make sure to save money while they are employed. Being employed means steady income; however, being an entrepreneur means your income is not steady. So, while you are working, make sure you are putting money aside and paying off as much debt as you can. You have to believe, and once you believe, you will achieve it. I have already pictured myself running my business full-time, meeting with clients, traveling, etc. Basically, living the life I've always wanted!

Strategy #7:
The Ultimate Sacrifice

We have covered a lot in this book thus far, but these last two strategies will require your undivided attention. In a prior strategy, we discussed how to be committed to the goal, but for this one, we will dive into what you will have to sacrifice in order to gain massive results in your business whether you are employed or not. "For whom much is given, much is required," and being an entrepreneur involves much sacrificing and compromising. So, if you are the type of person who can't see yourself sacrificing money, sleep, or going outside your comfort zone, then please keep working and save yourself the headache. Hell, writing this book cost me time, sleep, and money. Being an entrepreneur will challenge you in many ways, and only the strong will survive. You have to believe in things that you cannot yet see.

You have to compromise your comfort zone for the unknown.

You have to pray your way through stress.

Alot of times, you have to pray for a clientele that respects your business enough to pay your prices and pay on time. There will be a lot of sleepless nights and stressful days, but remembering your purpose will make the sacrifices much easier to bear.

When I started this journey, I didn't have much to sacrifice. I did not have a lot of money, and I stuck with my passion for writing so I didn't have to learn a lot on the process. Staying in my lane saved me at first, because I was comfortable remaining invisible while sitting behind the computer screen. That's why I loved songwriting so much; I did not have to be personally known or liked. I just needed people to like the artist or the lyrics. However, as I evolved as a writer, my comfort with sitting behind the screen was replaced with holding a microphone and standing on stage. Lights! Camera! Action!

Don't get me wrong, I love attention, but only from my man or children. Living my life publicly was different and made me uncomfortable because it subjected me to scrutiny, judgement, and having people voice their opinions and give suggestions. If you've read any of my previous books and know why I started writing, you would know I wrote so I would not have to publicly share my feelings. Interesting! What I ranaway from at age fourteen, I embraced at thirty-one. Even though I hate this requirement of my journey, I realize that, as a writer, sharing your story out loud is a part of the process. This, by far, is the most challenging sacrifice I continuously make to be who I am. In return, it has allowed me to connect with, learn from, and inspire others to follow their dreams.

Now, if you add being an employee, the sacrifice elevates. I used to tell myself that I would be further along in my business if I was not working full-time for someone else.

While I honestly believe that, I understood with the responsibility of having children, I could not sacrifice the money and health benefits that my job provided. So, instead of resigning, I used my time being an employee to learn, build, save, and plan for my departure. Plus, I did not want to quit my job and then have to return to the workforce because I hadn't properly prepared myself to be a full-time entrepreneur. Some lessons I was not ready to learn. Unlike many of you, I care about what people say about me. Many people can say I've failed, while others will talk about how I've conquered. But, what they won't say is that I was unprepared for anything. I will shut it down before I take that type of loss! I will never sacrifice my name!

After getting clear on what I wouldn't sacrifice, I did have to sacrifice many things to get to where I am today, not just as an entrepreneur, but as an employee and person. I can remember going to work exhausted after pulling an all-nighter writing my book, *Love the Real You*. I got to work at 6:30a.m. and started dozing off by 9:00 a.m. I had few sick or vacation days left to use, so there was no leaving work early for me. I drank about three bottles of Pepsi and ate a ton of chocolate, which did not help. When three o'clock finally rolled around, I flew out of work and drove ever so slowly home because I started dozing off again. When I finally made it home after picking up my son, I went straight to bed. Chris was in charge that night. I don't even remember hearing them play or talk. The house could have burnt down and I would not have known anything.

People assume writers have it easy. They think all we do is just sit and type. How wrong they are! Being a writer can be the most exhausting job ever. We create stories, dream up characters and become them, all while trying to keep a flow, a focus, and hold your interest with our words. For many, it takes time and a lot of long nights of writing, deleting, and rewriting. Then when your book goes through the editing stage, it involves more rewriting, creating, explaining, and discovering stuff that sometimes is not even true. However, for me and the kind of books I write, the experience can be challenging because I am reliving every headache, failure, pain, and situation that I vowed to forget just so you can learn and believe it is possible. The sacrifices are real, but I would not trade them for the world.

This journey of massive results and success came with a price. I know social media makes it seem like entrepreneurship is easy, accessible, and obtainable, but you must be willing to pay. Everyone will have to pay a different price, but trust me, it is not discounted nor is it free. So, as you invest monetarily to build your business, it is time to understand what you will have to pay emotionally, mentally, and physically for this lifestyle. Understanding this upfront is important because this is almost, if not the #1 reason, why many businesses fail. I would argue that most businesses don't actually fail due to lack of sales, capital, or experience. They fail because the founders underestimated the price they would have to pay before achieving all of those things.

By having an idea in advance of the price you will need to pay to reach a goal, you will be better prepared to deal with the challenges you will inevitably face during your journey to success. I'm not saying any of this to be negative or discourage you in anyway. Hell, I'm the first person to encourage almost anybody to become an entrepreneur and do what it takes to succeed. But, from reading this book, you also know I struggled in areas of business and life because I did not prepare for the rollercoaster ride that came with entrepreneurship. I was not ready when I hit those tough curves, the highs and lows, basically because I did not see it coming. Knowing what I know now, my goal is make sure you are equipped with everything you need if you're going to step into this ring. I need you prepared to fight, but not lose your life and lifestyle in the midst. So, I put together a list of some common sacrifices that entrepreneurs must be willing to lose or give up as they are building their dreams and working toward becoming successful.

- Sleep
- Social Life
- Relationships/Friendships
- Comfort Zone
- Sanity
- Mindless Entertainment

From this list, I will touch on social life and comfort zone. Having to sacrifice in these two areas really changed my perception regarding what's really important in life.

Social Life

Before I started writing, I was an active line dancer and active member of Zeta Phi Beta Sorority, Inc. and Order of Eastern Star, PHA of PA., as well as being a mother and daughter. However, while growing in my business and juggling all of my responsibilities, I had to step back so I could focus on my vision. Trust me, it wasn't easy. Nobody ever wants to just drop off the face of the earth when it comes to their life, friends, or things they enjoy doing. But, you have to understand that you can't be everything to everybody. Since you're only one person, you have to decide what is most important. Not to say your friends or social life aren't important, but you have to be more selective when it comes to how you'll spend your time. It had gotten so bad for me that I used to compare time to being money. Every free moment was a moment that I could utilize to be creative and build my catalog of books. All I wanted to do was write, create, and produce. But, when I finally came up for air, I was faced with a harsh reality. My phone had stopped ringing. I saw pictures online of my friends having fun without me. I started congratulating everyone via comments or text messages on their weddings, engagements, and new relationships instead of being present to celebrate with them. Just like that, I was alone and single. BUT, I had a great manuscript. A laptop substituted my personal life, and my social life had been reduced to giving out likes and commenting on Facebook, Twitter, and Instagram.

Whoever came up with the phrase "It's lonely at the top" knew what they were talking about. What baffled me was that I wasn't at the top of anything, though. I was still at the bottom grinding my way to the surface. So, here I am with a dream, no man to lean on and grow with, and friends who I could only celebrate with via social media. Was that the kind of life I wanted? I was paying dues to organizations but couldn't attend events because I was loaded down with writing assignments and book projects with deadlines. With this being my reality, there were many days when I wanted to quit. I was lonely and alone, but I had a dream. So, I had to choose between living a dreaming or having a social life. I could not believe I actually had to choose.

However, while I was still building, I realized this dilemma could be solved by managing my time better. I learned not to feel bad if I didn't work and write every second of the day. It was okay if I took two hours to enjoy a conversation with a friend or do some line dancing while hanging out. Now, even with the best scheduling, there will be some events and social gatherings you'll miss because of deadlines and other obligations, but at least you won't feel so lonely after the sacrifice.

Comfort Zone

Getting out of your own way is the biggest challenge for many entrepreneurs...well, people period. As defined, "A comfort zone is a psychological state in which things feel familiar to a person and they are at ease and in control of their environment, experiencing low levels of anxiety and stress." It is here that many people want to stay. Although, I'm someone who would rather work behind the scenes, being an entrepreneur and businesswoman have taught me that remaining behind the computer gets you nowhere. Even though with social media, one can post or tweet about their projects and businesses, people want to see you and hear your story. So, writing books was no longer enough. Speaker Charron Monaye had to come from out of the shadows and step into the light, even though it is not one of my favorite places. But, as we know, everything we want is on the other side of what we are not used to. We will never receive different results if we continue to do the same thing. Eventually, we have to change the process of what we do and how we do it.

International Speaker, Best-selling Author, and Coach Lisa Nichols once posted, "Your comfort zone is designed to keep you where you are, or worse yet, totally stuck. In order to move to that BIG, hairy, audacious goal, know it will be uncomfortable. Get comfortable with being uncomfortable! If you want something you've never had, you'll have to do what you've never done before."

And she's right! After digesting what she posted, I was forced to examine my whole life. How comfortable was I in all areas of my life? Back in 2013, I was comfortable with the following things:

- Living Paycheck to Paycheck
- Having Bad Credit

- Pleasing Others and Putting Their Ideas Over My Own
- Accepting What People Gave Me in the Name of Love
- Being Financially Irresponsible
- Being Just an Author
- Hindering My Growth for the Sake of Others' Happiness
- Not Believing in Myself Enough to Jump
- And the list goes on...

Just like many, *I was comfortable with not seeing progress; yet sitting and complaining about not growing.*

It wasn't until 2014 that life happened, and I'd had just about enough. You see, your business life is a reflection of your personal life, and your business will never grow if your personal life isn't on track. Don't get me wrong, I made money from 2009 to 2013, but I wasn't seeing a profit. My business was just as broke as I was, but I kept going. I spent money as soon as I got it, but didn't always see a positive return. When I was faced with an unexpected situation that I was unprepared for, I promised God and myself that if He got me out of it, I would value and respect His gift and my life better. As promised, my prayers were answered, and it came time to deliver on *my* promise. I broke all chains of fear and uncertainty, and I transformed my life one area at a time, all while growing in the Lord and regularly attending First Baptist Church of Crestmont. At that moment, I knew the only way I would change my mindset and place in life was by putting God First. The life I wanted was unfamiliar to me. The last time I had great credit was before I went to undergrad. So, with that, I knew someone other than myself had to be in control if I ever wanted to be free. When I turned everything over to God and allowed Him to lead me, I finally had the courage to live the life I prayed for. Stepping out of my comfort zone resulted in me:

- Establishing Great Credit
- Building an Emergency Fund
- Generating New Clients for My Writing and Coaching Programs
- Being Able to Take Vacations
- Generating a Profit in the Business
- Being Comfortable with Sharing My Story in Public
- Falling in Love
- Focusing on My Business
- Finding More Time to Be Social

Going from miserable to blessed took a lot of work and discipline, but in 2018, I am living my best life. I am happy as a person, and my happiness is transferring into my business. Are you living your best life? Are there areas in your life that you're comfortable in but you know you need to change? List them below.

1. _____
2. _____
3. _____
4. _____

5. _____

6. _____

Being an entrepreneur, you will experience loses and challenges, make sacrifices, and have to examine yourself in order to excel in business. Just keep in mind that sacrifices are necessary in order to help you get organized and provide you with a story worthy of sharing upon completion of your journey. Sacrificing may be hard, but it is only temporary.

Strategy #8:
Zero Capital & Bad Credit
What To Do???

This part is where I will need you to be super-sharp focused. Your understanding will either help you move forward or cause you to quit the journey way before your business has a chance to elevate. Being an entrepreneur has benefited my business tremendously; it provides the capital needed to publish books, invest in memberships, purchase business supplies, and travel to conferences. However, if you are not financial savvy, you will spend so much money on your business that you will bankrupt your life.

Money and I have not always been the best of friends. I saw money as something I made, not something that made me. So, it was nothing to spend it. But, as an entrepreneur, I had to learn how to budget, prioritize, and exercise more control when it came to what I spent my money on. This took years to understand. The way you think about money in your personal life will be the same way you manage your money in your business. Let me explain.

I was never taught the importance of money or had a clear understanding of savings, credit scores, investing, building wealth, or having an emergency fund. I always heard people say, "Put something up," but how much exactly was never defined. So, whenever I got cash or had available credit, I felt the need to spend it. Money was "burning a hole in my pocket" for sure.

In 2009, when I wanted to figure out this writing idea I had, I found myself broke, with no savings or credit. I was coming out of a marriage that nearly bankrupted me between being the co-signer on loans for my husband and using my credit cards to keep us afloat. I did not plan financially for my divorce because I never imagined it would come to that. However, when I ended my marriage, I was left with martial debt, with no way to pay it. To entertain the idea of pursuing my business dream, which would cost me more than what I had at the time.

At times, I wondered if I should let being broke stop me from going after what could be my legacy, or stop dreaming because investing in something that might not yield a profit could cost me more than I had to lose. Talk about risky behavior! But then my oldest son, Christopher, kept saying, "Mommy, you can do it." After listening to him, I proceeded very carefully. I figured if an eight-year-old had faith, then why was I doubting myself? What he didn't know was that there wasn't any money. All I had was a pen, composition book, laptop, and a bible. While healing, I needed to release my feelings, and writing kept me sane. My son co-signed the idea.

All I needed to do now was determine how I was going to publish the book. Since I knew I could not afford the expenses of self-publishing, I tried my luck at traditional publishing, but all I heard was...

"Poetry is hard to sell!"

"Thank you for your interest. Even though we enjoyed your work, we have to respectfully deny your request to be published."

"We are not accepting poetry at this time."

Denial letter after denial letter became the norm, and I was beginning to get discouraged. How did the greats, such as Maya Angelou, Nikki Giovanni, Sonia Sanchez, and many others, make a legacy writing and reciting poetry? Then I started questioning the messages of my poetry and my ability to write. *Maybe my writing is not black enough. Am I relatable? I* thought. *What am I doing wrong?*

As the rejection letters kept coming, I looked into vanity press publishers, hoping to find someone who would help me publish my book. Through the discouragement, I still held out hope for just one yes because I felt like another no would have been the end of my dreams all together. I had written and mailed so many query letters that I was mentally and physically spent. The gentleman at the post office wouldgreet me as soon as I walked in because it became my second home.

As I was connecting and pitching to vanity publishers, I got a call from Yulonda Brown of Purposeful Publishing. I wasn't sure if she was calling me to reject my request, but I prayed for a different result. She told me about her company, the services she offered, and the publishing packages that I could purchase. The pricing for her packages startedat $800.00, and I had less than $100.00 in my pocket. What was I going to do? Pay her to publish my book or decline the offer and keep waiting for a traditional publisher to say yes. What do you think I did? Before I tell you, let me breakdown the difference between the three types of publishing for those who may be interested in publishing a book.

- ✓ **Traditional Publishing** ~ A traditional book publishing company buys the rights to an author's manuscript. Part of the arrangement includes payment of an advance by the book publisher to the author to secure the book deal.
- ✓ **Self-Publishing** ~ Self-publishers own all their rights and receive 100% of the profit.
- ✓ **Vanity Press** ~ Vanity publishers offer publishing production services like editing and cover design that make them attractive to writers who want "one-stop shopping."

So now you see why I wanted a traditional publisher. All I had to do is write and they took the risk. However, since that was not working in my favor, I said yes and became a client under Purposeful Publishing. Not sure how I was going to pay her for the services, I started praying for a miracle or money to just fall from the sky. This was one of the many situations where I could have allowed being broke to prevent me from living out my dreams. Having a job made paying this expense doable, especially since I could pay it off in installments. Let me tell you, Pen Legacy or Charron Monaye would not be where we are today if it weren't for my investors Department of Veteran Affairs and Internal Revenue Service, along with cash advances from Capital One and Citibank. Chile! I owe them a big thank you! But, it took me years to understand that in order for me to grow as an entrepreneur, I needed to grow as a person. My financial portfolio from credit to cash on hand had to be on point, because if I ever needed to get business credit or a loan, my finances and credit score would be reviewed.

From 2010 to 2014, my paychecks, tax refund checks, and credit cards funded my business. I produced stage plays using my paychecks, developed and branded my business with my income tax refunds, and published books on credit. I was the type who would pay a credit card down and then run it back up, never really paying it to get out of debt. A vicious cycle that led me nowhere! I had no plan or process when it came to funding my business. Plus, I wasn't getting enough work or offering services that guaranteed me any profits. Every adventure was great for building what I envisioned, but it resulted in many restless nights and hungry days. Now my children never suffered directly because of my decisions; they didn't feel the pain of what I was going through. Half the time, they didn't know I had spent the rent money to publish a book and was praying steadfastly for people to buy copies so I could make some money back in order to pay the rent before the grace period expired.

The sacrifices and risky decisions I made in order to see my dreams come true are no different than those that many celebrities had to make in order to live out their dreams. If they would have allowed not having money to deter them from singing, acting, or performing, life for us would be boring. There would be no Taraji P. Henson, Kevin Hart, Dwayne "The Rock" Johnson, Brad Pitt, Steve Harvey, or Sylvester Stallone. These are some of the celebrities I found motivation in when my dream was bigger than my bank account. It wasn't until I read Sylvester Stallone's story and The Rock's quote that I realized my bank account did not define my legacy, and in order for this to work, I needed to build relationships, elevate my faith, and understand that being broke was a state of mind, not who I was. I knew my writing would one day return everything I invested plus more, but the only way to find out was to keep pressing forward. Still without a plan, I managed my household bills, paid for a catholic school education for my son, and cleaned up my credit. That last one was absolutely necessary, because with working for the government, your credit has bearing on you getting a security clearance. I often paid bills late in order for me to travel to different events or functions that would place me in front of the right people, and sometimes I sacrificed every dime I had to be there. There were two times that I traveled to events damn near broke because I knew the opportunity was worth more than what I had in my account and one that I could not miss.

The best part about both trips was that I had prepaid for the hotels, and since we drove to Atlanta, we didn't have to rent a car. In Los Angeles, I connected with my sorority sister Dominique, who took me out tour LA, Beverly Hills, Rodeo Drive, the Grammy Museum, and Universal Studios. Even though I love Atlanta, the experience in Los Angeles gave me the motivation to soar. When I returned home, I had that "eye of the tiger" mentality, and I declared that nothing would stop me. God had given me this gift of writing for a reason, and if I could survive in Atlanta and Los Angeles, I could survive the journey to see this dream come true. When I stood on that statement, it was like God made everything possible.

I got a refund check from school, which I used to pay off the balance owed to Yulonda so she could publish my book, *My Side of the Story*. I found a co-producer for my play, "Living Your Life", which premiered in Philly on September 26-29, 2012. It was like money was finding its way to me. My bills were paid on time; I didn't receive any more shut-off notices; and I slowly started rebuilding my credit. I still didn't have a savings account, but I was happy growing as a writer and building my life.

In the midst of the growth, I started learning about finances and credit. I kept hearing people talk about business credit and advising to keep your business and personal finances separately. While teaching myself about finances, I often came across the terms "emergency fund" and "snowball". However, it wasn't until I watched a show with Suze Orman that I put a halt on my business and started the process of getting my money in order.

During her interview, she asked a very important question that changed how I looked at money as an entrepreneur and employee. She asked, **"If you lost your job today, could you survive?"** Are you prepared with an emergency fund or at least 3 to 6 months' worth of expenses in savings so life can move forward as you regroup without you having to play catch up later? After letting those question marinate, I thought to myself, *It's time to put together a financial plan for Pen Legacy.* Frivolous spending was not allowing me to plan, prepare, or prosper in my personal life or in business. As soon as I made a dollar, I was spending it. If my only source of income were to end, my boys, myself, and my business would be screwed. So, in corrective mode I went.

I pulled my personal credit report from all three credit bureaus to see my credit worthiness on paper. Then I created services through Pen Legacy that would generate revenue. I set up a savings account and set an allotment that would automatically deposit into my savings account from my paycheck; this is what I used to start an emergency fund. I even started being picky concerning which events I would attend. Prior to this, I was paying for and attending everything I could just to say I was there or to get my product in front of people. I had no strategy and I had no plan! But, I had a phone and my selfies were on fleek. I had all kinds of pictures with celebrities, but neither them nor that picture endorsed my brand. I had the picture, though.

Even though I don't regret investing in my dreams, I knew it was time to be smarter about my choices, because in spite of who I thought I was becoming, I was still the mother of two children, and the last thing I wanted was for us to end up homeless or have to move back in with my mother if my job folded. As I continued to educate myself and strategize my finances, I decided it was time to take a break from Pen Legacy. So, from 2014 to 2015, I took a step back from the business to get my money in order. I no longer wanted my job to be the sole investor for Pen Legacy. It was time for the business to fund itself; it was time to separate my life from the company and rebrand Pen Legacy. I am grateful for what I was able to do for my business because of my job, but it was time to be legit and smarter about things.

I joined Lexington Law and had them repair my credit. I read financial books by Nicole Lapin and Dave Ramsey. I worked overtime to pay off the credit cards that I had previously used for Pen Legacy expenses. I opened a separate bank account and started saving, and I started saving the correct percentages for retirement. In a little over a year, my credit score rose from within the 500's to the mid 700's. I was becoming a financial guru and focused on living financially free. It was during my learning period that I realized finances, in addition to having a strong clientele, were the key to business growth. You can't operate, fund, or brand your business without money. A lot of the things you need to even start a business require money, but it took me five years and a lot of money to realize there's a better way to do this. Once I got my personal finances in order, it was time to build a financial portfolio for the business. I applied for a business credit card, checking account, tax identification number, and repriced all my services. This way, the business could finally operate as its own entity. This all happened in 2017.

You are probably asking yourself, "Why did it take her so long?" Good question! It took me so long to get aligned with my finances because, like most entrepreneurs and small business owners, I was more *eager* than *educated*. We are so eager to want people to support our journey instead of first planning the journey. My biggest mistake as an entrepreneur was not being smarter with my finances. I failed to plan and capitalize on opportunities, and I failed to understand my target audience and identify a marketplace. I was creating and investing without outlining how I was going to make my money back! I was one of those people who created just because I could, not because it was a need. Thus, as to why I had to hit the brakes and rebrand, but now I must say my finances are great. Pen Legacy is truly operating as its own entity, and as I stated before, 2017 marks the first year I made a profit and as an employee made six figures. When you have a plan, you have progress! Finally, I am prepared to write my resignation letter!

ENTREPRENEUR FINANCIAL TIPS

So how do you take my mistakes and apply them to your business so it doesn't take you as long to achieve greatness? Here are a few tips you can use that I now carry with me to help me maintain my financial success.

- ➢ It is essential that you keep your personal finances and business finances separate. Make sure you are paying yourself a salary (rather than paying your personal bills) out of the business finances.

- ➢ Track all your personal expenses. Create an excel spreadsheet and track all expenses. This will make you conscious of what you spend and it will help you create a daily budget.

- ➢ Hire outside help, such as a bookkeeper or accountant, to assist you with your business finances.

- ➢ Plan and strategize how you will spend and receive money. Before making any purchases, ensure it is something that is needed and will help generate revenue.

FUNDING YOUR BUSINESS

I want to offer you some tips on how to fund your business other than relying solely on your paycheck. Knowing what I know now, your paycheck can be used to contribute to the business, but it should not be the only means. Here are six ways to gain capital to fund your business:

1. Secure a Small Business Administration Loan
2. Seek Money from Family and Friends
3. Get a Microloan
4. Use a Business Credit Card
5. Pitch to an Angel Investor
6. Crowdfunding

PERSONAL FINANCES CLEAN-UP

If you need to fix your personal finances, here are some helpful steps on how to clean them up and elevate your credit score.

Step 1: Set Up a Filing System for Your Personal Finances

Step 2: Create (and Stick to) a Budget with the Help of a Budget Calculator

Step 3: Set Up Payment Reminders or Automatic Bill Payments

Step 4: Balance Your Payments with Your Paydays
Step 5: Evaluate and Pay Off Your Debt
Step 6: Start Saving Money

7 STEPS TO GETTING BUSINESS CREDIT

We all understand how to get and build personal credit. Pay your bills on time; don't create too much debt. But, business credit? That often seems like a mystery for many small businesses. The process of getting business credit is in fact similar to building your personal credit profile, only everything is in the name of the business. Here are seven steps I have used to gain and maintain my business credit.

Incorporate ~ The first thing to understand is that to build business credit, you must separate your business and its finances from your personal finances. By creating a separate entity, you allow your business to have a legal structure and credit rating apart from, and different than, your own.

Get an Employer Identification Number ~ Issued by the IRS, an EIN is the business equivalent of a Social Security number. If you don't have one, get an EIN from the IRS.

Get a DUNS Number ~ Issued by the main adjudicator of business credit, Dun & Bradstreet, a DUNS number is your business's credit profile number.

Open up two bank accounts ~ The first should be a standard checking account. Create it using the business name, EIN, DUNS number, and business address. Second, open up a savings account or CD tied to the business checking account. Deposit some money in it.

Obtain vendor credit ~ Once you have all of your numbers and accounts in place, you can start the actual process of building your business credit profile. See if your local office supply store will give your business a small credit line in the name of the business. Maybe one of your suppliers or vendors will do the same.

Get a loan ~ Use that bank savings account or CD to obtain a small loan from the bank, again in the name of the business. By securing the loan with the business savings account, you 1) give the bank every reason to say yes to your loan request, and 2) begin to build business credit by showing you are responsibly repaying a business loan.

Pay on time ~ Repay all loans and credit on time and in full.

I know this chapter was full of my experiences, teaching, and coaching, but the sooner you realize how important your finances are to your business, the faster you can get in alignment to write that resignation letter. Before we move forward, get clear on what you need help with when it comes to your finances. Write your needs below.

_____

_____

_____

_____

_____

_____

_____

_____

Now that you've jotted that down, determine if you need to take a break from building so you can concentrate on fixing your finances or if you can proceed forward. Remember, we are looking to gain massive results and eventually resign, so it is imperative that your finances be in order! Business revenue and personal income should not be used collectively. Take it from me, I learned this lesson the hard way. Until you can get to a point of establishing separate entities, then unfortunately, I would recommend you keep working. Or at least find more streams of income to help fund everything you desire without you going bankrupt or becoming homeless. The goal is not to make the same mistakes as I did, but to learn from them and reach your goals in a less drastic way.

"I Want to Quit My Job"
Entrepreneurial Conversation...

Annette J. Morris, M.A. Professional Mental Health Counselor, Certified Life Coach, Motivational Speaker, Published Author, Entrepreneur and Business Consultant. "You will get all you want in life if you help enough people get what they want" is the Zig Ziglar quote Annette has modeled her life after. Her professional career is focused solely on helping others to either accomplish their goals as an entrepreneur or in life as a whole.

The owner/lead consultant of Goal Getter, LLC., she has published three books: *Conquering the EneME, Live Free: Creating the Streams to Live Your Dreams*, and *Everyday's a New Day: Daily Positive Affirmations for Positive Daily Living*. She also hasan empowerment CD entitled *Live Free*, which teaches steps to financial freedom. Of all that she's accomplished in life, she's most excited about being saved and a child of the Most High God.

Contact info:
Email: Ajmorris@goalgetterforever.com
Phone: 504-452-0110
Website: www.goalgetterforever.com

Tell us about your business? What problem does it solve in our communities?

The name of my business is Goal Getter LLC., which is a for-profit service and product based business entity that provides consulting and coaching services that empower individuals to live their dreams. We help aspiring entrepreneurs to convert their passion to profit and existing entrepreneurs to expand their businesses. Some of the services we provide are 501c3 development grant writing, business plan development, t-shirt printing, and book publishing services.

As an entrepreneur, what are some of the challenges you face? What strategies have you mastered in order to stay in business?

Everyday I wake up as an entrepreneur is a challenge. Why? Because there are no set paydays for me; however, I grind to make everyday a payday. I wake up in the morning, read my scripture, say my prayers, and command my day to generate at least a hundred dollars for me. In commanding my day, which is the faith part, I take action to assure my works line up with my determination. I hustle from sun up to sun down to ensure not only that my business is successful, but that the businesses of those I work with are, as well. My purpose in life is to help others live in theirs. I've mastered the art of not sleeping. (LOL!) Entrepreneurs burn the candle at both ends and straight up the middle. Most entrepreneurs I know operate on very little sleep. Consistency and determination outside the time restraints of 9 a.m. to 5 p.m. is the only way to get it.

In regards to branding, how important would you say it is when it comes to a business? What tips can you provide to those who are building their company?

Consistency in branding is key! Decide on a look that's catchy but also represents your brand. Design your logo and marketing material accordingly, then make sure it's in the face and eyesight of as many people as possible who meet the criteria of your target population. Not branding and marketing is the equivalent to keeping your business a secret--it's pointless to have a business and keep it a secret. Branding and marketing is essential to the growth and success of any business.

Knowing what you know now about entrepreneurship, what are five things you would have done differently before opening your doors?

When I took the leap of faith, it wasn't because I wanted to. I can remember God speaking to my spirit, telling me it was time to take the leap. I was neither physically nor financially ready, but I knew I had to be obedient. So, I was, and it has allowed for many opportunities that I know I would have never encountered had I not been obedient. If I had not been called to this, there are several things I would've done differently before becoming a full-time entrepreneur. Some of those things are:

keeping my job longer and using my earnings to take care of personal matters, create a sizable savings and invest some into my business. I would've followed this routine for at least a year. This allows enough time for someone to transition into entrepreneurship comfortably and with a cushion. Also, I would've created a 1-,3-, and 5-year plan for the business to help me better prepare for slow seasons. Lastly, I would've created a plan that captures the streams of revenue the business has the potential to generate, so when it's a lean season for one avenue of revenue, we can easily tap into another. It's so much I've learned on this journey in the past six years; I wouldn't trade it for anything in the world. Experience has been the best teacher.

With all of the ups and downs of business, how do you remain committed to your business? What advice would you offer to someone who has a business but is struggling with clients, profits, and motivation?

Always remember your WHY! When your WHY is clearly defined, you will never lose sight of the reason you went into business. My *why* is spiritual, biblical, and physical. The Bible says we are to leave an inheritance for our kids. As an employee, there was no part of the company I could leave to my kids because the company wasn't mine for them to inherit. As for Goal Getter, LLC., its services and products are in my name, and upon my demise, it will transition over to my kids.

It's Time to Execute!

Now that you have learned my 8 Entrepreneurial Strategies for Massive Results While Employed, I want you to use this section to set goals, journal about your progress, and celebrate your milestones. If you have already completed a section, write it within the section and make sure you celebrate your win!

1) Understanding the Purpose

What is your business's purpose?

_____

_____

_____

_____

_____

_____

_____

_____

_____

_____

_____

_____

_____

2) Executing The Business Set-Up 101

Who is your target audience?

_____

_____

_____

_____

_____

_____

_____

_____

_____

_____

Jot down your business plan.

_____

_____

_____

_____

_____

_____

_____

_____

_____

_____

_____

How will you fund your business?

1. _____

_____

2. _____

_____

3. _____

_____

4. _____

_____

What business structure did you select for your business?

_____

What is the name of your business?

_____

What is your Tax ID number?

_____

Branding Strategy:

_____

_____

_____

_____

_____

_____

_____

_____

_____

Marketing Plan:

_____

_____

_____

_____

_____

_____

_____

_____

_____

Write a 60-second pitch for your business.

_____

_____

3) Remaining Committed to the Goal

1st Goal:

_____

_____

_____

_____

_____

_____

_____

_____

_____

_____

_____

2nd Goal:

_____

_____

_____

_____

_____

_____

_____

_____

_____

_____

_____

_____

_____

3rd Goal:

_____

_____

_____

_____

_____

_____

_____

_____

_____

_____

_____

_____

4) Your Employer is your First Investor, Capitalize on It!

What will you use your paychecks for?

_____

How can your job provide leverage for your business?

_____
_____
_____
_____
_____
_____

5) How to Balance Time and Family with No Time Left in a Day

How will you balance your time?

_____
_____
_____
_____
_____
_____

What are the theme days for your business?

_____
_____
_____
_____
_____
_____

6) Self-Care Leads To Great Wealth

1st Goal:

_____

_____

_____

_____

_____

_____

_____

_____

_____

_____

_____

2nd Goal:

_____

_____

_____

_____

_____

_____

_____

_____

_____

_____

_____

3rd Goal:

_____

_____

_____

_____

_____

_____

_____

_____

_____

_____

_____

7) The Ultimate Sacrifice

What will you have to sacrifice?

_____

_____

_____

_____

_____

How does it make you feel?

_____

_____

_____

_____

_____

_____

Are you committed to your business?

_____

_____

_____

_____

_____

8) Zero Capital & Bad Credit…. What To Do???

Credit Score: _____ out of 850

Business Credit Score: _____ out of 100

Net Worth:Assets_____ – Liabilities _____ =
_____ (Net Worth)

1st Goal:

_____
_____
_____
_____
_____
_____
_____
_____
_____
_____
_____
_____

2nd Goal:

_____
_____
_____
_____
_____
_____
_____
_____
_____
_____
_____
_____

3rd Goal:

_____

_____

_____

_____

_____

_____

_____

_____

_____

_____

_____

_____

"I Want to Quit My Job"

Entrepreneurial Conversation...

Na'Kesha Johnson, better known as the Serial Hustlerpreneur, is a Jane-of-all-trades. She's a Network Marketing Beast, Direct Sales Guru, Published Author, Motivational Speaker, Mentor, Leader and Empowerment Coach from Brooklyn, New York. She's also the CEO and founder of V.O.G.U.E Visionaries, a women's empowerment group that offers encouragement, support, accountability, and positive reinforcement to one another, as well as celebrate each other's successes.

Na'Kesha is a strong believer in GOD and credits all her success to Him. Because of her faith, resilience, tenacious spirit, and the power of prayer, she is turning everyone of her passions into paychecks!

Contact info:
Phone: (619) TEA-CHIC
Website: www.nakeshajohnson.com
@nakeshasnetworks on all social media platforms.

Tell us about your business.

Well, I'm known as the "Serial Hustlerpreneur" because I run several online businesses, along with a few side hustles. I've been in the Multi-Level Marketing (MLM) industry for 18 years. My current MLM company is a direct-sales company that pays five different ways. I'm also an affiliate with a funded proposal marketing system. This allows me to generate DAILY income, create instant cash flow, and build my email list, as well as build my primary business on the back end. Some of my side hustles include doing hair, event coordinating, hosting ladies' nights, bartending, party promoting, and selling just about any and everything. Those are things I like to do for fun, so why not get paid for it? One thing I know how to do is make a dollar out of fifteen cents. Living in Brooklyn, New York, having multiple streams of income is a MUST.

When did you know it was time to leave your job and pursue your business full-time? What made you say enough is enough?

I've always had a hustler's spirit, so I knew entrepreneurship would be my path at some point. It just came sooner than I expected. When I had my son at age 19, I settled for a few dead-end J.O.B.s (Just Over Broke). I did data entry, some retail, and worked in corporate America for about five whole minutes, and I hated it. I hated the fact that I had to pretend to be something I'm not and everyone was brown-nosing their way to the top. One thing all of those jobs had in common was that my checks were already spent before they were cashed. There were some days I had to choose between paying my phone bill or buying groceries. Either way, I was screwed because I had to wait another two weeks before I got paid again. And guess what? That check was already spent, too. I was literally living paycheck to paycheck and barely getting by. I just couldn't go on like that.

Most people say you should have at least a year's salary saved prior to quitting your job. Did you have that much saved? How did you prepare financially?

I would love to paint you this beautiful picture of how I had money put aside and was ready to make all types of investments in my career and future, but that wasn't the case. An opportunity was presented to me, and I was put in a position where I had to take advantage of it. It was now or never. I wasn't prepared mentally or financially for what would come. I didn't even have that fifteen cents to turn into a dollar. (LOL!) All I had was my little bit of faith that's big as a mustard seed. Still, I knew I had to take that leap. Everyone from my family to my friends thought I was crazy. *I* thought I was crazy. But, I knew I no longer wanted to work for someone else; therefore, I had to take advantage of this opportunity.

During your journey as an entrepreneur, what have you had to sacrifice so you can build your business?

My biggest sacrifice was time away from my son. When building a business, it requires a lot of time and energy. I was in a training program that eventually led to me opening my business, but it wasn't paid training. I was doing management training for half of the day and field work the other half. The money I made on the field was split between feeding my son, bills, and other responsibilities. The majority had to go towards my business. So, I wasn't away from home during the average nine-to-five timeframe that others work. I was gone all day, and my son was only two years old. I felt like I was failing as a parent, not to mention the negative backlash. People called me a no-good mother and accused me of neglecting my son. It was so bad that I almost lost custody of him. So many people were talking about me and laughing at me. It was mentally and emotionally overwhelming, but I knew I had to make the sacrifice worth it. And I did.

Being an entrepreneur, we know there can be a lot of challenges and struggles, from getting clients to staying relevant in your field. What challenges have you faced and what steps did you take to overcome them?

Challenges is an understatement. One of my biggest challenges was opening a new business in New York City at the start of a recession. I was running a sales office, and people were not thrilled about the idea of selling products out on the street and working on commission. Fortunately, I have a gift of making people fall in love with sales, and in order to do that, I had to lead by example. So, I went back to the basics. As the boss, my workers saw me dressed up and in heels, conducting interviews, doing orientations, and running my business. They also saw me as a leader. I wasn't scared to throw on a pair of jeans and sneakers and hit the pavement again. I could've stayed behind my comfortable desk and sent my sales team out with one of my good trainers, but I knew I was my best trainer. It gave my workers the confidence that if I can do it, so can they. That's where a lot of business owners go wrong. They get comfortable and stop working. They think the business is going to run itself, not realizing in order for that to happen, you have to practice the same work ethics that you did in the beginning. While other businesses were suffering and their sales were plummeting, mine were skyrocketing. I made sure my following week was better than my last. I threw fun contests and gave out incentives. I always showed up!

What advice would you give someone who is an employee, but wants to seek entrepreneurship full-time ? What are five things they should have before making this jump?

A very important piece of advice that I will give is before walking away from your job, make sure you are pursuing your dream of being an ENTREPRENEUR and not a WANNAPRENEUR. Many people are in love with the idea of being their own boss but are not willing to put in the work required. I'm going to break down five things I think are very important to have before making this jump.

1. **MINDSET** – Although it may sound cliché, you must possess the right mindset in order to succeed. You're going to face unexpected obstacles that will come your way. Learn to fall in love with your challenges. You're going to have to always be coachable and open to learning new things to master your craft. If you don't take this seriously and go into it with the right mindset, you might as well stay at your job. You'll never be successful being a "broke" know-it-all.

2. **SELF-DISCIPLINE & SELF-MOTIVATION** – You're going to quit mentally a thousand times. Just make sure you don't. You're going to wake up some mornings tired, sluggish, and not wanting to get out of bed. Make sure you get your butt up. These are the things we feel working a regular jobs, but we still show up to work for someone else. Why not have the discipline to do it for yourself?

3. **BUSINESS PLAN**– What do you want to do and how are you going to go about doing it? You have to do your research and have some type of marketing strategy. Have an idea of what the startup cost will be to launch your business. The goal is not just to be an entrepreneur, but to be a SUCCESSFUL entrepreneur.

4. **INCOME PRODUCTING ACTIVITIES (IPA)** – Once you leave your job, you'll no longer have that guaranteed paycheck coming in. You have to do IPAs, and you have to do them daily. You need money coming in for your personal necessities, and you're always going to be putting money back into your business, especially when you first launch.

5. **BACKUP PLAN** – You can think you're doing everything right as an entrepreneur, but you still have to be prepared to face circumstances beyond your control. Anything can happen. It's just a part of life. What if you face a sudden illness? What if your initial plan just doesn't work? I didn't have a backup plan when I first started out, but if I did, it probably would've taken some unnecessary stress off of me. I still don't know how I did it. But, what I have learned is you have to work smarter and not harder when it comes to entrepreneurship.

When Can I Write My Resignation Letter?

The purpose of this book was to offer you strategies to build your business, generate profits, and elevate your personal life while employed so you are mentally, financially, and emotionally, prepared once you take that leap of faith. While many celebrate entrepreneurship, I want you to be prepared for what's to come and the trials you will have to overcome. The entrepreneurial world is not for the faint at heart. Entrepreneurs must be motivated, creative, versatile, risk-tolerant, driven, a visionary, and open-minded. In addition, your personal life must be in order, because as we already discovered, your business is a reflection of your life. Therefore, you must have a positive and strong mindset about life and purpose.

So when is the right time to write your resignation letter? Some people will tell you when you have at least six to twelve months' worth of your salary saved; others will say to put your trust in God and quit today! Honestly, I suggest you hand in your resignation letter only after you:

- Have a plan
- Start seeing results
- Researched the market and realize there is a need for your idea
- Have a stable customer base or marketing plan
- Have evidence of profits possibility

- Have money saved, and
- Have a clear understanding on your responsibility and mission as a business owner and entrepreneur

If you read through the eight strategies, answered the coaching questions honestly, did your research, and possibly hired a coach to help you through the building and planning process, you can probably start drafting your letter as soon as you finish reading this, especially if it will give you the motivation to stay focused. But, continue treating your employer as your investor until your business is able to pay you as the founder and employee.

If you are an entrepreneur and not on your own payroll, there is no room for quitting just yet. How can you afford to quit a job that pays you to work for a job (your business) that can't? You still have bills, children, expenses, a lifestyle to maintain, and a net worth to build. It takes money to build the business you want, and you will lose money while building it. So, why not use this time to build your company while continuing to get paid from your employer. Another thing, make sure you are pricing your services and products accordingly, and stay abreast on your market. Break free from your fears, challenge yourself to try new things, partner with others, and take advantage of Facebook Live, Periscope, and YouTube to help you promote. Remember, it is not enough to just post a comment. People want to hear your story, have access to you, and feel like they are a part of your world.

In addition to the eight strategies I provided, I want to offer you six more things to consider before resigning. The more prepared you are, the less likely you are to struggle or become discouraged.

1) Know exactly how much money you need to afford your life.

Do you truly know how much money you spend each month? Tracking your spending behavior can be an eye-opener. What's more, knowing exactly where your money goes each month is the best way to understand if you have the financial means to quit your job and where you should make cuts, if necessary. Start by calculating the exact amount you earn after taxes. Don't forget to deduct any automatic transfers going to your 401(k) or other funds. Next, spell out your monthly expenses. Creating a spreadsheet might help. Include your bills and any ongoing debts that must be covered. Look for ways you can cut back in order to make quitting your job a reality, then figure out what you can save each month. For example, getting rid of cable TV could save you about a hundred dollars a month, if not more.

2) Expect the unexpected.

Stuff happens. Maybe you'll need a root canal the second you drop your dental insurance. Maybe your roommate will move out, and you'll have to pay the full amount for rent until you find another roommate to split it with you. Without a steady income, it's harder to absorb unexpected costs in addition to your basic living expenses. That's where an emergency fund comes into play.

In addition to your "quit my job" fund, which you should use for everyday expenses, it's wise to have a separate fund dedicated to emergencies only. Creating separate accounts can help you focus on your goal and get there faster. An emergency fund should have another three to six months' worth of living expenses in it. For example, if you need $2,500 a month to live on, you'll need a total of $30,000 for your "quit your job" and emergency funds combined. If you can save $1,000 a month, it will take you two and a half years to save that much. Save $1,500 a month, and you'll get there in a year and eight months.

If your account earns interest, the time that it will take you to reach your savings goal will be a little shorter, but not by much. Most online savings accounts pay around 1% interest, so it won't cut the total time drastically. (You'll have earned just $365 in interest in 30 months if you earn 1% interest, for example.)

3) Do you have any evidence that your idea will fly?

Too many entrepreneurs start companies without doing enough research or asking enough hard questions to make sure their product or service is something that people actually want or need. One way to try out your business without quitting your day job is to build your company on the side, in your spare time, until you know for sure it can survive in the marketplace.

4) Create a game plan.

Once your goals are in place, it's time to put your action plan in motion. How would you support yourself if you went out on your own? Do some research to support your idea. The first sketches of a game plan could become a rough draft of your business plan. Make sure to create target dates for bringing your idea closer to fruition, and eventually, it will include the day you leave your day job!

5) Create a worst-case scenario plan, as well.

Have a 'worst-case scenario' plan. If your business fails and you run out of money, what happens? More than likely, you'll get another job in the workforce. So, plan for this possibility by keeping in contact with key people who might have work for you should you ever need it.

6) Leave on a good note.

Quitting your job without giving at least a two-week notice, could be the worst move to make prior to your departure. Yes, you are leaving to start your own venture, but you cannot be sure that it will be a success or that you won't need something from your old company one day. Leave without burning any bridges and you may be able to cash in a favor one day. Your old employer may even send clients your way if they feel you are a trustworthy businessperson

How to Write Your Resignation Letter

To help you out, here's a step-by-step template to use.

Part 1: The Basics

There's no need to sugarcoat or get creative in the beginning; just state the position you're resigning from and the effective date. While you probably shared with your boss your reasons for leaving, you don't need to describe them here. Keeping it simple is perfectly fine.

Part 2: The Thank-You

Next, it's always a good idea to thank your employer for the opportunity, describing some of the key things you've enjoyed and learned on the job. And, yes, this is true even if you're thrilled to be leaving. Remember, you may need these people for a reference down the line, and leaving on a good note will leave a lasting (positive) impression.

Part 3: The Hand-Off

Finally, state your willingness to help out with the transition in your resignation letter. You don't need to go into great detail (and definitely don't promise anything you can't deliver), but a couple of lines stating that you'll ensure a smooth wrap-up of your duties will show you're in the game until the very end.

Resignation Template

Dear [your boss' name],

Please accept this letter as formal notification that I am resigning from my position as [position title] with [company name]. My last day will be [your last day—usually two weeks from the date you give notice].

Thank you so much for the opportunity to work in this position for the past [amount of time you've been in the role]. I've greatly enjoyed and appreciated the opportunities I've had to [a few of your favorite job responsibilities], and I've learned [a few specific things you've learned on the job], all of which I will take with me throughout my career.

During my last two weeks, I'll do everything possible to wrap up my duties and train other team members. Please let me know if there's anything else I can do to aid during the transition.

I wish the company continued success, and I hope to stay in touch in the future.

Sincerely,
[Your name]

Obviously, feel free to adjust this a bit based on your experience and your company culture. Then submit it using the standard procedures at your company.

Use the lines below to draft your resignation letter. You can either prepare it for your departure or use it to motivate you through the process.

_____

_____

_____

_____

_____

_____

_____

_____

_____

_____

_____

_____

_____

_____

_____

_____

_____

_____

_____

_____

_____

_____

_____

Entrepreneurial Resources

Small Business Administration:
https://www.sba.gov/
Small Business and Self-Employed Tax Center:
https://www.irs.gov/businesses/small-business-and-self-employed-tax-center
Dun & Bradstreet:
http://www.dnb.com/duns-number/what-is-duns.html
Business Health Insurance:
https://www.healthcare.gov/small-businesses/
Health coverage For The Self-Employed:
https://www.healthcare.gov/self-employed/coverage/
United States Patent & Trademark:
https://www.uspto.gov/
Copyright:
https://www.copyright.gov/
Business Credit:
https://www.nav.com/business-credit-scores/
Entrepreneurial Coaching:
www.penlegacy.com
Business Structures:
https://www.irs.gov/businesses/small-businesses-self-employed/business-structures
Elevate Your Personal Brand in 2018:
https://www.entrepreneur.com/article/306068
Free Scheduler & Booking Site:
https://simplybook.me/en/

ABOUT THE AUTHOR
CHARRON MONAYE

Like many young girls, Charron Monaye kept a journal, except hers consisted of poetry which she never expected to give a voice. Only out of necessity did she put it on paper. To hold it inside was too overwhelming. Finally releasing her thoughts, even if only on paper, was empowering.

That defining moment led to her becoming an Award-winning playwright/author/coach/entrepreneur and writer.

After overcoming multiple panic attacks at the ripe young age of thirty, Charron had to learn how to give her pain a voice while not blaming herself in the midst. She had to remove toxicity, manage overwhelming financial setbacks, and muster up the strength to leave an unhealthy marriage, all while raising her children. In the midst of it all, Charron Monaye adapted a new sense of survival while being ready to open up about losing everything…and finding peace in the process.

To find her voice, power, and strength, she released her first book of poetry, "My Side of the Story," in 2010 under Purposeful Publishing, LLC. It was so raw, so transparent about her marriage and divorce, that it was adapted into a stage play entitled "Living Your Life" and featured in the Black Theater Festival in Washington D.C. with actress D'atra Hicks. Realizing the power of her words, Charron created her literacy company, Pen Legacy, in 2015, which offers self-publishing, script-writing and writing services, and writing/empowerment coaching.

Since then, Charron Monaye has written 10 books, (co-author of 2), and written/produced 3 theatrical productions. She was a former content contributor for CNN iReport and The Philadelphia Association of Paralegals. In addition, her works can be found in eleven books and poetry anthologies across the world. In 2017, she received a Doctorate of Philosophy (Humane Letters) from CICA International University & Seminary. Just recently, she had the opportunity to hone her writing skills by studying under television producer, screenwriter, and author Shonda Rhimes and NAACP Image Award Author Victoria Christopher Murray.

Compelling women, men, and girls with her story and equipping them to succeed, Ms. Monaye continues to inspire others to use their voice to stand in the power of their greatness through her talks, workshops, and keynote addresses.

Charron has a Bachelor's of Arts in Political Science from West Chester University, Master's in Public Administration from Keller Graduate School of Management, a Certificate in Paralegal Studies and Life Coaching. Charron is an active member of Zeta Phi Beta Sorority, Incorporated and Order of Eastern Star.

Contact Info:
Author Website: www.CharronMonaye.com
Email: info@penlegacy.com
Business Website: www.penlegacy.com

Facebook & Twitter: PenLegacy
Instagram: iamcharronmonaye
LinkedIn: Charron Monaye , MPA

Share The Knowledge

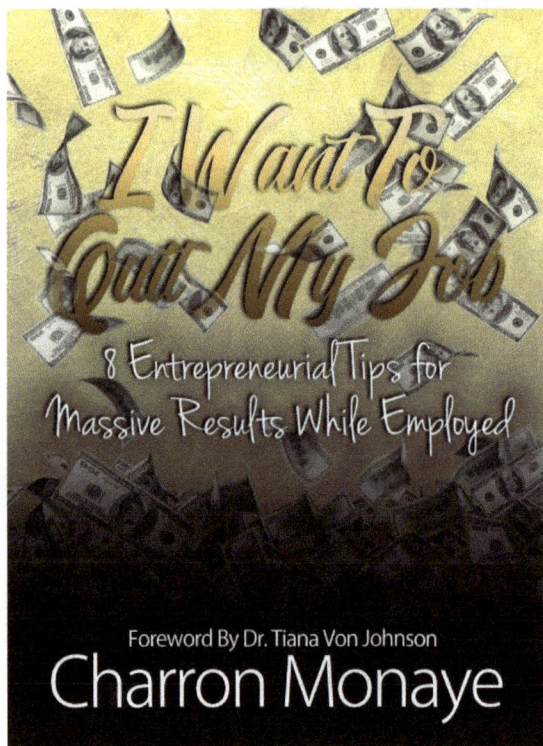

Retail Price $24.99

Special Quantity Discounts

7-20 Books	$17.95 each
21-99 Books	$15.95 each
100-499 Books	$12.95 each
500-999 Books	$9.95 each
1000+ Books	$6.95 each

To Place An Order Contact: info@penlegacy.com

Books Published By Pen Legacy Publishing

Journals/Guides

Boss Moves Start With You: 2018 Self-Reflection Journal & Vision Planner by: Briana McKnight

2018 Legacy Journal & Planner: A Planning Tool for your Freedom & Future by: Charron Monaye

Maximizing Your Tax Refund Made Easy! by: Khristina Barnes

I Matter Journal by: Charron Monaye

Book Compilation

Bruised, Broken, and Blessed compiled by: Charron Monaye & Shontaye Hawkins

Inspirational/Non-Fiction

STOP Asking for Permission & Give Notice: How To Accept & Attain Who You Are Without Validation by: Charron Monaye

Respect Your Choices: Finding Balance in Success by: Vaughn McNeill

Love The Real You: Uncovering your "WHY" & Affirming You're Enough by: Charron Monaye

Let Me Tell You Like I Told Myself: Love's Truth Never Changes by: Summer Willow Fitch

Fiction

Leonard Smith by: AJ Harrison

Memoirs

The Shadow In My Eyes by: Deborah Rose

The WoodShed by: Jaguar Wright

The Black Blood In My Heart by: La'Mena Marie

Poetry

UnBreak My Heart: From Scorn to Finding Love Again by: Charron Monaye

My Side of the Story: From a Woman Waiting to Exhale by: Charron Monaye

Business/Entrepreneur

I Want To Quit My Job: 8 Entrepreneurial Strategies for Massive Results While Employed by Charron Monaye

Books are available on Amazon, Barnes N Noble, Books A Million, Wal-Mart, Penlegacy.com

PENLEGACY
PUBLISHING & SCRIPTWRITING COLLECTION

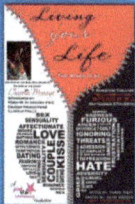

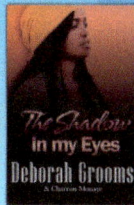

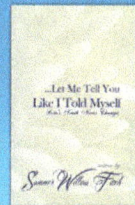

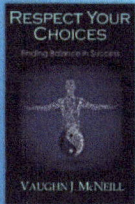

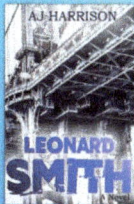

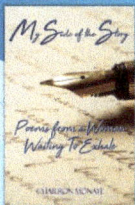

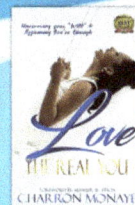

220

www.ingramcontent.com/pod-product-compliance
Lightning Source LLC
Chambersburg PA
CBHW051849090426
42811CB00034B/2273/J